The Joy of Bocce - 2nd Edition

by

Mario Pagnoni

authorHOUSE™

1663 LIBERTY DRIVE, SUITE 200
BLOOMINGTON, INDIANA 47403
(800) 839-8640
WWW.AUTHORHOUSE.COM

First published by AuthorHouse 12/09/04

ISBN: 1-4184-0717-8 (e)
ISBN: 1-4184-0716-X (sc)

Printed in the United States of America
Bloomington, Indiana

This book is printed on acid-free paper.

First edition published by Masters Press 1995

Table of Contents

Chapter 9 Bocce Courts We've Known & Loved – A Pictorial 179

Chapter 10 Organizing A League/Promoting The Game...195

Chapter 11 Tournament Play & Rules 217

Chapter 12 International Play 235

Chapter 13 Bocce & The Special Olympics 265

Chapter 14 The Best Of The Joy of Bocce Weekly 277

Acknowledgments ▰▰▰▰▰▰▰▰▰▰

First and foremost, I must thank my father-in-law, Gennaro Daniele, who gave me my first set of bocce balls. This gift led to a love affair with the sport. After decades of baseball, basketball, jogging and five knee operations, bocce has become more appealing to me than ever.

Heartfelt thanks go to my son James, whose excellent photographs complement the bocce text so well. Thanks also to my son Joseph, who helped with the photo demonstrations and to my wife, Carmela, who put up with the disaster area that our backyard became during the bocce court construction. My good friend Joe Austin deserves high praise and my undying gratitude for the many hours that he put into our backyard court construction.

To all our ezine readers (*Joy of Bocce Weekly*) who submitted photos from bocce venues everywhere, I thank you for sharing those great snapshots of our game. Too numerous to mention all of them here, I gratefully acknowledge the most frequent contributors. Leonard Hickey graciously submitted numerous photos of bocce play at his marvelous outdoor court in Wilbraham, Massachusetts. Michael Grasser (Michigan), Tom McNutt (Washington), Dave Brewer (California) and John Ross (California) are bocce lovers of the highest order. They go out of their way to submit photos of the bocce courts they encounter on their travels.

Many thanks to all who have submitted tips on technique, strategy, and tactics to improve play. Included throughout the text are tidbits of bocce wisdom from Michael Conti, Dr. Angel Cordano, Rico Daniele, Phil Ferrari, and Michael Grasser.

For their input and objective criticism of early drafts of the manuscript my gratitude goes out to Donna Allen and Ken Dothee of the United States Bocce Federation, Rico Daniele of the Wonderful World of Bocce Association, and Phil Ferrari of the World Bocce Association. Special thanks to Jennifer Smith and Rosemary Picarillo who analyzed the manuscript from the perspective of a non-player.

Finally, many thanks go to the good people at the original publishing house, Masters Press, including Tom Bast, Holly Kondras and Heather Seal. They embraced my idea for a book on bocce and, with great skill, took the project to completion.

Preface

Bocce, though already catching on rapidly in this country, would really take off if it got the proper exposure. Hopefully this book will help. I'm not talking about it flourishing as a tournament event with complicated rules, state-of-the-art equipment, and high-powered authorities running (or ruining) the sport. I'm referring to a simplified recreational version that can be played by anyone almost anywhere. This game doesn't require great strength, stamina, quickness or agility. You don't need cat-like reflexes or the hand-eye coordination of an NBA backcourt man. Men and women as well as boys and girls of all ages can participate and enjoy the sport, making it as competitive or as laid back as they desire. And it is well suited as a game for the countless physically challenged individuals worldwide because anyone who can roll a ball can play. Best of all, you don't need expensive equipment. And, played as described here, you don't even need a court - your back yard or neighborhood park will do nicely. You can play recreational bocce on grass or dirt, on level or uneven terrain - even at the beach (on the shore or on sandbars during low tide).

Bocce suffers from an image problem in America. People see it as an "old fogies' game" played at social clubs. The word bocce conjures up images of cranky old coots competing on customized outdoor courts. Arguing and kibitzing (sometimes even cursing - usually in Italian) and generally having a great time, these old-timers seem engaged in some sort of geriatric lawn bowling. It looks about as exciting as watching cactus grow in the desert. But it is a wonderful game, full of skill and strategy - one that requires finesse as well as some occasional brute force. This book attempts to dispel the misconceptions about bocce, and aims to promote it as a lawn game that is the ideal recreation for family cookouts, picnics, and other get-togethers. In addition, this book will help guide those who may want to take the game to the next level, whether it be the social club level, tournament, or international play. Most of all, our goal is to get the word out on what has been called "the best kept secret in sports", bocce.

This edition dedicated to our friend and bocce MVP, Armando Iannalfo, who succumbed to cancer in 2004. Armando loved bocce, even scheduling his chemotherapy treatments around our league play.

Chapter 1
A Brief History Lesson ▬▬▬▬▬▬▬

(Relax -- there won't be a test!)

Bocce is an ancient game, its origin and evolution obscured by the mists of antiquity. The waters are further muddied by the fact that its development is intertwined with that of other bowling games. It is often unclear whether a historical reference refers to lawn bowls, bocce, or bowling. The more I attempted to research the history of bocce, the more I realized that there is no definitive history of the sport. What follows is less a history than a mixture of fact, conjecture, lore, and outright guess (don't look for footnotes and references). The lack of detailed documentation, however, makes the tale no less fascinating or intriguing.

Sir Flinders Petrie, emeritus professor of Egyptology at the University of London, unearthed an Egyptian tomb from 5200 B.C. bearing evidence of a bowling game played by young boys tossing balls or polished stones. Other Egyptian wall paintings and vases also appear to depict bocce-like games in progress. Some historians have gone as far as to call bocce the ancestor of all ball games.

It is believed that thousands of years ago inhabitants of Pharaoh's Egypt became the first bocce players (must have been a welcome diversion from stacking pyramid stones). Later, Roman legionnaires played with naturally rounded rocks or perhaps coconuts brought back from African campaigns (must have been a welcome diversion from stacking corpses of the conquered). Bocce may have derived from an ancient Greek exercise of throwing balls of varying size for distance. This sound mind, sound body ideal of the Greeks was right up the alley of the Romans, who modified the activity, tossing and rolling the balls along the ground toward a stationary target.

Bocce spread throughout the Middle East and Asia. Historians believe that the Greeks latched onto the game at around 600 B.C. (as evidenced in the painting and sculpture of the period) and introduced it to the Romans. The Romans probably took it on the road via their world conquest and spread the game Johnny Appleseed style. During breaks in the Punic Wars, soldiers selected a small stone "leader" and threw it first. Then they rolled, tossed, or heaved larger stones, with those coming closest to the leader scoring points. All of this appears to have been easy exercise and a pleasant change of pace from the stress of battle.

The Egyptian game became bocce in Italy, and was altered slightly to become boules in France and lawn bowls in England. It is easy to imagine the early games being played with spherical rocks or even coconuts (later, artisans would use hard olive wood to carve out balls). The name bocce is derived from the Italian *bacio* meaning kiss. The idea is to kiss, snuggle, or otherwise get close to the object of your affection – the pallino (target ball).

Eventually, people from all walks of life played bocce and bowls. The young, the old, men, women, scientists, artists, royalty -- people of all stations enjoyed the sport. It is said that Caesar Augustus was partial to the game. Some medical experts even suggested that playing the game prevented rheumatism. In 1319 A.D., King Charles IV of France banned bowl games for all but the nobility, because it supposedly diverted attention from more important tasks such as preparing for war and practicing archery. Edward III of England followed suit in 1361. In 1511 King Henry VIII imposed a similar ban on his subjects' (commoners and soldiers) lawn bowls.

He reasoned that the activity might divert attention from a (necessary for national defense) and lead to gambling and moral decay. A further act of 1541, not repealed until 1845, forbade commoners to play except on Christmas (and then only in their masters' house and in their presence).

By 1519 bowling games became public diversions played in Flanders, Holland, and Belgium. As we have seen, the games were banned at various times in Italy, France, and England and were once even condemned by the Catholic Church citing a "pernicious gambling influence." Clearly, legislation failed to kill or seriously subdue interest in the sports. They flourished into Elizabeth's reign where bowls assumed prominent social status. Over time however, bowl games became increasingly associated with taverns, drinking, and gambling and became unfashionable.

In 1658, one Puritan offered the following confession after succumbing to the temptation of forbidden bowling: (Excerpted from *The Complete Handbook of Bowling* by Oscar Fraley. Prentice-Hall, Inc. 1959.)

"To those concerned, I hereby say, I should not make confessions which are likely to be read from this page at some future time by public eyes but my conscience is troubling me, so I seek this way to ease it. The weather is tantalizing warm, but I was tempted to do what I have refrained from doing before. This game of bowls has bewitched me, I fear. For I played it today and for funds. Yet, I was fortunate, for the bet was £10. Woe unto me! My fellow Puritans will be shocked if they hear of this, but the more reason for my confession. I like the game, my own ability to win, and the fine folks I met on the greens. May this confession do my soul good."

The ball games' lore suggests that Sir Francis Drake, when told of the rapidly advancing Spanish Armada, insisted on finishing his game before setting out to resist the enemy. And Italian tradition has it that playing bocce in the streets resulted in bruises to the legs of passing noblemen. This served to bring much attention to the sport among Italian nobility and led to it becoming a favorite pastime of the aristocracy. Giusseppe Garibaldi, who is more widely known for unifying and nationalizing Italy, is also credited with popularizing the sport as it is known today. Bocce had its ups and downs historically -- periodically gaining and losing popularity. In 1896, the first Olympiad was held in Athens, Greece. Bocce hit the international scene then and is holding on tenaciously today.

When Italian immigrants brought their game to America in the late 19th and early 20th centuries, it was a regionalized version of the activity. Just as there are similar yet somewhat different dialects throughout any country, there were similar yet varying ways of playing bocce. Each court constructed in the United States met the specifications of those used in the immigrants' area of the "old country." Similarly, each area used the regionalized rules from their part of Italy. Bocce is and has remained a remarkably resilient game, surviving and growing despite these problems.

Spectators have always taken to the sport, with kibitzers seemingly a necessary element of bocce. Everybody seems to have an idea of how the next shot should proceed, and few are reluctant to share their counsel. It is reminiscent of the classic *Mad Magazine* spoof on Little League baseball. As a youngster is sprinting toward third base, the parents and coaches are wildly calling out instructions. "Score, Score, Score!" says one adult. "No --Stop, Stop, Stop at third!" calls out another. "Go Back to second!" orders yet another. "Tag up! Tag up! Tag up!" and "Slide! Slide! Slide!" are still other commands from the stands. Like Little League parents, bocce's armchair generals are evidence of the game's abiding appeal.

In Italy and in the early days of bocce in the United States, women and children were discouraged from playing. This game was the domain of men. It may have begun to die out because men did not share it with women and the younger generation. Its resurgence today is due to the fact that play is no longer confined to Italian adult males. It has escaped its ethnic roots and has become a game for all people of all ages. A movement is on today to construct courts in public parks. This is a major step toward spreading the game to more and more Americans. Extending the game from the private sector (social clubs that require membership fees) to the public sector also provides the opportunity to get outdoors and play in the fresh air with family and friends. In Martinez, California, affiliates of the United States Bocce Federation maintain 15 outdoor courts. You can even get pizza delivered to your "door" by telephoning and specifying your court number.

Played in Italy since before the Caesars, bocce has survived the Fall of the Roman Empire and the threat of fascism. It has evolved to a tournament sport carrying ever-increasing cash prizes and luring corporate sponsors. Undoubtedly it will thrive and continue to flourish. This is testimony to the enduring appeal of an activity that evolved in different parts of the world, is played somewhat differently from country to country, yet whose basic idea is the same. Let's see who can roll, toss, or otherwise deliver their bocce balls closest to the object ball. Bocce, played widely today in Italy, Australia, South America, and other countries, is about to explode in the United States.

Taking The Game On The Road

Jim Vaughan, sales manager extraordinaire for the Bargetto Winery (3535 North Main St., Soquel, CA 95073 – www.bargetto.com) has "taken the game on the road". According to Vaughan, "I introduce Bargetto wines to buyers and wine consumers with bocce as the sporting background. Some of the wine & bocce venues were on the traditional surface, while others were improvised. For instance, we played on the carpet of a French bistro in Singapore, a putting green on the island of Kauai, inside a warehouse in Seattle and alongside horse stables in Tucson. The fusion of wine tasting, food, music and a relaxing (often very competitive) bocce tournament creates an appealing social dynamic."

Bargetto's Cal-Ital
signature wine

Vaughan's bocce & wine tasting participants began asking numerous questions about the game (especially about its history). His research lead him to *Storia Delle Bocce In Italia E Nel Mondo* (*The Story of Bocce in Italy and the World*). With the editorial assistance of Bargetto Wine Club Director Ms. Dana Sheldon, Vaughan wrote two newsletters reviewing the first volume of this three-volume masterpiece.

The historical trilogy, published in Italian by Signor Daniele Di Chiara (and thirty years in the making), isn't available for purchase. Di Chiara's effort (as historian for the Federazione Italiana Bocce in Rome, Italy) was primarily for the "love and prosperity of the game."

Vaughan, after having sections of the texts translated into English, reveals that Di Chiara acknowledges the "...murky anecdotal evidence..." that surrounds bocce's origin. Following bocce through time, the author cites more conclusive evidence in the well preserved ruins of Pompeii (destroyed by Mt. Vesuvius in 79 A.D.).

"Inside one room were nine spherical stones, all perfectly round. One of the stones was considerably smaller, the target ball. This room became known as Bocciodromo (The Bocce Room)."

It is common belief that Greek colonists introduced bocce to the Roman Legions. Di Chiara explains, "The Romans developed a better quality of the game of bocce. They took it from simple manifestation of force to proof of ability. Not a matter of distance but how the stone would make the other one move."

According to Vaughan "The Greeks were shot putting, and the Romans gave it a degree of skill and wit. This version was introduced as the Legions marched, conquered and expanded the Roman Empire. It was not only popular with the soldiers during their free time, but enjoyed by local artists, the noble elite, politicians and the common citizenry.

By the Middle Ages, most European countries were playing some form of bocce (also referred to as 'boules'). To this day, France and England have the closest cousins to bocce: pétanque and lawn bowling."

Vaughan concludes that "Daniele Di Chiara and his team of editors and researchers have truly captured the passionate spirit of the ancient game."

Listen to the voice of Englishman Sir Thomas More in this 1543 proclamation:

'Servants, peasants, citizens…people of all classes are exhibiting extravagant taste in food and clothing. Bordellos abound, especially those that also provide taverns or brew houses. There is deplorable waste of money in games of chance such as darts, cards and bocce… Are these games not merely incentive for theft? We must liberate the people, then, from these wicked ruinous ways. Redeem them from sloth and send them back to their agricultural and wool markets. Give them back to the satisfaction of doing something useful…those with time on their hands get into trouble.'

And here is Di Chiara's and Vaughan's take on the Sir Francis Drake anecdote:

"Most of the bocce literature mentions yet another Englishman in the game's history. If there were ever a Dream Team captain for this time period, Sir Francis Drake would be the leading candidate. Regarded with great respect in the English navy as a daring and bold navigator of the seas, Drake was also quite passionate about bocce. Described in the book is a scene of Drake engaged in a heated game with fellow officer Admiral Lord Howard. With the seemingly invincible Spanish Armada rounding the entrance to Plymouth Harbor, Drake is quoted as saying, quite calmly: 'First we finish the game. We have plenty of time to worry about the Armada.' Drake won the contest against Admiral Howard and then soundly crushed the Spanish fleet."

Nailed Boules – Nineteenth Century France

Quite by accident I learned of France's nailed boules, a fascinating part of bocce history. Recently a bocce buddy of mine took me to visit an antique dealer in Salem, Massachusetts.

"Come take a ride" he said. "This dealer has a box of metal bocce balls you might like."

Thinking they might be the small metal pétanque balls, I resisted.

"No," my friend insisted. "These are about the same size as the bocce balls we play with every week."

Reluctantly, I tagged along on this lazy Saturday afternoon. Good thing I did! In a cardboard box underneath some old furniture in the back of this quaint shop in the city of the infamous witch trials were…balls. Not just balls, but hand crafted works of art with what appeared to be individual nails pounded into some kind of wood center. The craftsmanship was fabulous. A couple had numbers on them configured by different colored nails. Two were absolutely beautiful…a kind of mosaic of different color metals.

I purchased the lot of them, took some photos and posted them on my web site, hoping that some reader would enlighten us about what I now had in my possession.

The author's collection

Frank Pipal, a boules (pétanque) player from Sonoma County, California came through with flying colors.

"What you've got is a bunch of very nice Boules Lyonnaises (or volo balls if you like). They are widely collected and desirable - which all the antique dealers in France know. They will have been made in France in the years prior to the appearance of the "Integrale", the first all metal boule.

There were many styles of nail work. The core is a ball of boxwood root.

9

The word bocce, (bocca in Provencal - the language of southern France) comes from the Latin for Boxwood - buxus. The numbers are simply to identify the balls. Often the balls carry the initials of the owner (made to order), or designs.

There's a village in the south of France which is famous for its nailed boules (Aiguines). The trade died out in the thirties with the advent of the Integrale in bronze and then the JB all steel boule.

From the Wegner collection   *From the Wegner collection*

Aiguines was famous for the small boules used in the Jeu Provencal and later in Pétanque. They are usually "fish-scaled". The big balls were probably made closer to Lyon and Grenoble and other centers of that style of play."

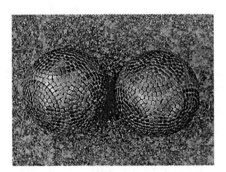

The author's favorites
(nailed mosaic)

Besides educating us about this fascinating art, Frank did us a great favor by alerting us to a fabulous web site on the subject.

"What you really need to do is go to Herbert Wegner's web site and see what is probably the most beautiful collection anywhere."

http://perso.wanadoo.fr/herbert.wegner/

WARNING – visit this site at your own risk. If these nailed boules pique your interest, you will likely spend great stretches of time here, keeping you from chores or other tasks (all the more reason to visit).

There are some "must see" pages with spectacular images. The excellent, well-crafted site gives details of the history of this fascinating part of bocce's past. "Different nails" outlines the various nailing techniques. "BOULES" displays images of 80 magnificent nailed boules. "Old pictures+cards" highlights postcard/picture reproductions that positively enthrall.

From the Wegner collection

A Word On Bowls (Lawn Bowling)

"What sport shall we devise here in this garden, to drive away the heavy thought of care?" Queen Isabella queries in Shakespeare's Richard II. "Madam, we'll play at bowls," responds her handmaid. Lawn bowls is a ball-and-target game similar to bocce, in that players roll balls toward a stationary object, but is played on a closely cropped grass lawn without side and end boards. The eight-to ten-ounce jack is rolled down the course and competitors use three-pound bowls made of wood, rubber, or composition material to try to score points. These bowls are not round but biased; they are elliptical and weighted on one side. The weighting was originally accomplished by loading the ball with lead, but now is done by making one side more convex than the other. When rolled, this bias causes the ball to curve like a ten-pin bowling ball (perhaps lawn bowls is the precursor of that game). An interesting wrinkle to this game is that as each ball is delivered, the player's rear foot must be on, or above, a small, strategically placed mat.

New York's Bowling Green is a reminder that bowls was an important recreation for early settlers. George Washington's dad built a bowling green at Mt. Vernon in 1732, and the game enjoyed great popularity until the Revolutionary War, after which it became dormant for the next 100 years or so. George Vanderbilt and John D. Rockefeller had private bowling greens on their estates, and Walt Disney hosted bowling friends at his Palm Springs home.

A Word On Boules (Pétanque)

Boules, jeu de boules, or pétanque are names for the French version of bowls or bocce. Although the game is played in many countries, boules is as closely associated with France as bullfighting is with Spain. It is usually played on sand or gravel with metal balls that are smaller than bocce or lawn bowls. Like bowls, the game is played without side or end boards on an area called a *pitch*. The object ball (beut or cochonnet) is so small (on the order of a table tennis ball) that the game is difficult to play on grass. Even closely cropped lawns tend to obliterate it from view. As in lawn bowls, the rules require players to take their shots from a designated area (often both feet within a circle drawn or painted on the ground).

Kissing The Fanny

Pétanque, it appears, is responsible for the tradition whereby losing bocce or boules teams are obliged to "kiss the fanny." Kissing fanny is the punishment for losing a game without scoring a single point. ALL players defeated by a shut-out have to kiss the fanny with the winning team players serving as witnesses. This is why, wherever boules is played, a figure of a fake fanny is fervidly flaunted. Whether a painting, picture or ceramic sculpture, the unhappy losers are obliged to peck, in public, the usually generous cheeks of the image.

Legend has it that the tradition started in France's Savoy region. The first Fanny (a common first name in France) was a waitress at the Café de Grand-Lemps, circa World War I. A gentle and compassionate soul, she would allow customers who had lost at boules without scoring a solitary point to kiss her on the cheek.

One day it was the village mayor who had been "skunked" and came

*Campo di Bocce
(Los Gatos, California)
carries on the
"kiss the fanny" tradition*

14

Pétanque players Cannes, France (Wegner collection)

to collect his kiss. Reportedly, there was "bad blood" between the two, and intending to humiliate the mayor, Fanny stepped up onto a chair, lifted her skirt and offered him... her fanny! The mayor was up to the challenge and, two loud kisses echoed through the café...the beginning of a longstanding tradition...

A Classic Case Of One-Up-Manship

The three ball-and-target games of bocce, boules, and bowls are classic contests of one-up-manship. If you can roll the ball six inches away from the target, I can draw to within five. Such activities have had enormous appeal, especially with the element of strategy and team competition are added to the mix. And 7000 years of staying power is a pretty good endorsement. If we consider bocce, boules, and bowls variations of the same game, that game must be classified as one of the largest participatory sports in the world today.

Chapter 2
The Game ▰▰▰▰▰▰▰▰▰▰▰▰▰▰▰▰

The Reader's Digest Version (read this chapter and you're ready to play - come back later and read the rest of the book)

Bocce is a simple yet elegant game. Although I love the game as it is played in courts across the country and throughout the world, I'm partial to the simplified, backyard version - the one that can be played by men and women, boys and girls of almost any age. The one that can be learned in minutes and played almost anywhere. The one described in this chapter.

Bocce's Appeal

I am an unabashed promoter of bocce. I bring a set of bocce balls along whenever I travel or attend outdoor parties. Starting a game with family or friends on a patch of grass or dirt, we invariably draw a crowd. Inquiring people want to know - how do you play? - What's the object? Are the balls just like bowling balls? Can I hold one to see how heavy it is? Most often they've heard of bocce, but have seldom if ever played. After a five-minute explanation and a quick try, they're hooked. They want to know where to get their hands on a set of bocce balls and, chances are good that they'll become bocce buffs.

Played the way we'll describe here, bocce is a gentle pastime, an entertaining recreational endeavor. Females should be pleased that in this age of male dominated sports, bocce is suited equally to both sexes. Co-ed games are not only possible, but desirable. The tendency with backyard bocce is to include everyone - husbands and wives, neighbors, children - all want the ball in their court.

In subsequent chapters we'll take you through the terminology, examine the strategy, and tell you where to get equipment. We'll even describe how to construct a court of your own (if you have the inclination and the place to build one). But for now, here are the basics - enough for you to begin playing today.

Getting Down To Basics

A set of bocce balls consists of eight large balls and one small ball called the pallino (Italian for little ball). The larger balls are roughly the size of a grapefruit (the size, weight and composition vary with manufacturers and some offer a variety of sizes and weights to suit the individual player - see Chapter 6 - The Equipment). Two teams compete against each other in this ball-and-target game. Each team gets to roll or otherwise toss four of the larger balls toward the pallino (also called the jack, pill, or object ball). Each team's four bocce balls are of a different color or are otherwise marked for differentiation. For example, a set might consist of four red balls, four green balls and a yellow pallino.

The object of the game is to score points by getting your team's balls close to the pallino. Novices think it advantageous to hit the pallino, but this may or may not be true. In any case, you don't score by hitting the pallino, but by directing your bocce balls closer to it than your opponents can. After both teams roll all of their balls, the frame or round is completed, and only one team will score. You score one point for each ball that is closer to the pallino than the closest ball of your opponent (to the pallino). Score one point if your ball is closest to the pallino, two points if you have the two closest to the pallino, etc. In this way, you can score up to four points in each frame.

One point   *Two points*

Three points   *Four points*

The game can continue to 11, 12, 15, 16 or even 21 points (or another score that is mutually acceptable to the participants). We suggest games of 12. This is sufficiently long to make for fair competition, yet doesn't keep the on-deck players waiting too long (there are always on-deck players). Some tournament directors schedule games to 12 but increase the winning score to 15 or 16 in the finals, presumably to ensure that the better team wins. (The shorter the game, the better the chance of an upset.)

In lawn bowls they sometimes play a set number of "ends" (frames or rounds) instead of playing to a set point total. They might agree, for example, that the leader after 15 ends is the victor.

An elderly woman from Florida told me that her group played tournament games to 21. "Wow!" I said. "Those games must take forever."

"Well," she countered, "We have a lot of time at the retirement center."

Although not very common, we sometimes hear of areas where they play "deuce game" – the winner must win by two points. Rick Bushong, webmaster for the Crockett Bocce Club (California) web site says that "the two point rule makes for some exciting finishes in close games."

Note: Although there are variations to the rules played around the country, a serious attempt to establish a standard set of "open" or "recreational" rules has been made by many groups. Of course, these rules have differed slightly (and sometimes not so slightly) from group to group. Rules for international bocce play are well established, having been used worldwide for years. These will govern future Olympic games, and are far more disciplined and complicated than the recreational rules discussed here (see chapter 12 for international rules). Until now there has been no standardization for bocce play in North America. After almost two years of corresponding with players and bocce organizations via email, snail mail, fax, telephone and face-to-face, I have compiled and am publishing here for the first time the North American Open Rules - see chapter 11 for complete text.

The game is best played with one to four players per team. In the one-on-one version (singles), each player rolls four balls. With two players per team (doubles) each participant tosses two balls. And the four vs. four game allows one shot for each team member. This last method of play has its ups and downs. On the plus side, it involves eight players at once. On the negative side, you only get one shot per frame (you do more watching than playing), and this prevents you from getting a feel for the terrain on any given lie.

With four-player teams there are two different formats. You can roll one ball each, as described earlier, with all eight players playing from the same starting location. After the frame or round, the eight players walk to the other end of the court or play area and begin play back in the opposite direction. Of course, in your backyard or playground area (sans court) you can play in any direction you choose. We prefer to roll the pallino right from where we just completed the round, rather than picking up the balls and moving to a new starting point.

The alternate format is to station four participants (two from each team) at either end of your play area. With this method, each participant tosses two balls and stays at his end. We are basically dividing the teams of four into two subgroups of two. When the group from one end plays, the other group members act as coaches, fans, and most importantly - measurers. We keep a cumulative score - if you score two points and then your partners score two points, you are ahead four to nothing. Critics of this style claim that "you are only playing half a game" and "it reduces the exercise (walking) that bocce provides."

Two-on-two (doubles) is my favorite way to play bocce. You get two shots, allowing you to "go to school" on your first ball, and you get a partner allowing for greater camaraderie. After each frame you walk to the other end, pick up the balls and begin play in another direction.

You can also play with three players per team (triples). You have to decide who on each team will get the extra ball each frame. Perhaps you could rotate it. You could even keep the six active by stationing four players at one end (two bocce balls each) and two at the other (four balls each). But with six or more players I prefer teams of two in a kind of round robin format. Play games of 12 and have the on-deck team have a burger or act as measurers or referees. Depending on the skill of the participants, games last anywhere from 15 minutes to an hour. Another option with three- or four-player teams is to utilize two sets of balls so that each player can deliver two balls. Three-player teams would require 6 balls per team (12 balls in play), so, theoretically a team could score six points in one round. Similarly, two four-player teams with two balls each make a total of 16 balls in play (with the possibility of eight points per frame). Caution - things are likely to get a little crowded.

To begin the game, teams must agree on who will toss the pallino first. You might flip a coin, throw fingers in the old odds-evens game of our youth, or come up with another alternative. The game starts when one player tosses the pallino to any position he desires. In our backyard bocce version there is no minimum or maximum distance that the pallino must be tossed (unless the players agree to such restrictions beforehand). Now the person who tossed the pallino tosses the first bocce ball, attempting to get as close to the pallino as possible. While you don't get points for hitting the object ball, a shot that nestles right up to pallino, obscuring it from the next player's sight, is very tough to beat. In any case, once the first ball is played, that team has the advantage - they're closest. Now it is up to the opponents to roll their bocce balls until they win the point - by getting closest to the pallino - so far. This may take one, two, three, or all four balls. Play continues in this manner (sometimes referred to as the nearest ball rule) until all balls are played and one team scores one, two, three, or four points. To recap - when Team A has the point (has the closest ball, or is "in"), they step aside and wait until Team B beats that point (has the "in" ball). Team B rolls as many balls as needed to "outlag" Team A's ball. If they can do it with one ball, fine. Now they will "hold the point" as some players say, and Team A has to try to beat Team B's point. Obviously, a good first shot could force the opponents to use two, three, or even all four of their balls. This puts the team with a good first "point man" (or woman) in an advantageous position.

Note: after the initial toss of the coin and subsequent first round of play, the team that scores always rolls the pallino. Also, the team rolling out the pallino must play the first ball as well. Teammates may decide among themselves who will toss pallino, or they may alternate this privilege, but the honor must go to someone on the team that scored.

Sometimes a shot is so close that it is too difficult to outlag. In this case a team is likely to try to knock it away with either a fast rolling shot called a *raffa* or a direct hit on the fly called a *volo*. In either case, successfully knocking away a close ball opens up the play for you or your teammate to come in for the point. As you will see in subsequent chapters, this movement of opponents' balls, your own team's balls, or even the pallino makes for an infinite variety of possible tactics.

Order Of Play Within A Team

In singles play each player tosses four balls, so play proceeds quite simply. If your opponent is "in", it's your shot next. But with two or more players per team you need to decide which player will roll when your opponents have the point. You might agree ahead of time that "I'll throw the first two balls and you throw the last two." In four-person teams (one ball to be played by each) you can also preset the order by designating a first, second, third, and fourth shooter. But most often teams will discuss strategy while the game is in progress and agree, "You are better at this type of shot - why don't you try it?" The only restriction is that whichever team has the point (has the nearest ball) - a player from the other team must play next.

On bocce courts, lines are marked to indicate how far forward a player may stand when rolling a ball. Since courts are lined by sideboards, this limits players' lateral movement. But there are no such restrictions in an open backyard. Usually this doesn't present a problem - players agree to take their shots from the same general area. Sometimes disagreements arise when a number of balls are in front of the object ball and the shooter doesn't have a clear view of it. He takes a step to his right. Then another. And another. Clearly there has to be some limit or he could circle completely around to the other side of the balls. Try to get everybody to play from a couple steps left or right of the spot from where the object ball was rolled into play. If this doesn't work out, put down a welcome mat and instruct all to place one foot on the rug when taking their shots.

The Playing Surface

Although bocce is played worldwide on enclosed clay, stone dust or synthetic courts, you can play on almost any surface. You need only a dirt or grassy area of 30 to 70 feet long by at least eight feet in width. It may be perfectly level, extremely hilly, or anywhere in between. In fact, sloping areas on the playing field make for interesting shots involving "reading the green" as in golf. Generally, good golfers make good bocce players. They're skilled at gauging just how far a ball might break to the right or left and they tend to have a soft touch (smooth release of the ball). Basketball players with good shooting touch also tend to make fine bocce players. They know how to let the ball roll off the fingertips imparting a forward spin to the ball (12 o'clock to 6 o'clock rotation).

Just as the enclosed court introduces a dimension of playing off the side and endboards, playing on the green (or dirt) adds a nifty element. You can toss the object ball in one direction, play a round, and then proceed in any other direction. You might roll the pallino near the base of that willow tree and see if you can navigate over, around, or through the exposed roots. Or you could place it near that chain link fence (acting as a kind of sideboard) and try to carom shots, first kissing the ball off the fence, then steering it neatly next to the object ball. The possibilities are endless.

In backyard lawn bocce, most people play a kind of anything-goes style. One player told me about spirited games played at family cookouts. In one particularly competitive contest the pallino got bounced up into the air and right into a trash can. One family member acting as referee offered... "I'll get the pallino out of the trash and we'll start the frame over." This was met by a chorus of "Like hell you will!" Both teams then attempted to gain the point by tossing balls into the barrel on the fly.

Measuring For Point

Measuring to find out which ball is closest to the pallino can present problems. At the most noncompetitive level of recreational bocce, players often concede a point on a close call or just agree to call it a tie (no point scored). At the opposite end of the spectrum, participants use state-of-the-art measuring devices complete with calipers capable of discerning fractions of an inch.

The first rule in determining the nearest ball is to move up to the area of the pallino. Sometimes a ball that appears to be inches away when viewed from the foul line is actually several feet away when viewed up close. And the angle can fool you. For example, Team A's first roll may end up about even with, but a foot or two to the right of the pallino. Team B's shot is straight on, but apparently six inches or so short of the pallino. Before Team A plays the next ball, they should get a better look by walking up to the balls and surveying the situation. Quite often the ball that appears to be six inches short is actually several feet short. Of course, this trip to the pallino is unnecessary if you have someone acting as referee.

When determining point, always move up to the pallino and stand in the proper position. From the foul line, often one ball appears to be "in", when it is actually "out" when viewed from the proper angle.

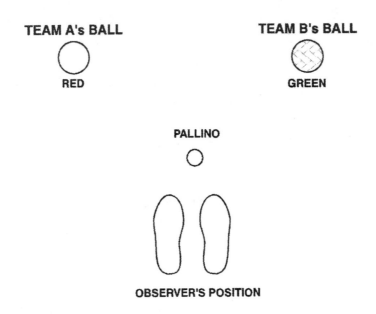

Observer's correct position

A second important rule for determining which ball is in is to stand behind the object in a kind of straddling position with the balls that are in contention in clear view (see photos previous page and drawing above). Experienced players can determine which ball is in for the point even when one ball is only a fraction of an inch closer than another.

My family and I have enjoyed backyard bocce for many years measuring only by eye or with feet, hands, and fingers. This nifty system really works! Start at the pallino and place the heel of your foot against it. Take care not to displace the pallino. Take "baby steps" straight toward the ball you are measuring, carefully placing the heel of one foot directly in front of the toe of the previous. When you get too close to the bocce ball to squeeze in another foot, keep your front foot in place, and kneeling down, use your fingers as more precise units of measure. In this way we can tell that the ball that is three feet and four fingers away is out, and the one that is three feet and three fingers away is in.

When the distances to be measured are smaller than feet and awkward for fingers, or require a bit more precision, we have used twigs, pieces of string, and other easily accessible objects. A telescoping radio, television, or car antenna works very well if it is sturdy and straight. A standard tape measure is helpful, especially for very long measurements. We have seen some neat homemade measurers, too. One creative guy on the bocce circuit taped a car antenna and a presentation pointer together so that they could be opened telescopically in opposite directions. "A single antenna is good" he claims, "but it's just not long enough for many measurements." Finally, there are some precise measuring devices on the market which we outline in Chapter 6, The Equipment.

Some Points On Measuring For Point

1. Stand by the pallino and see if you can make the call by eye. Give opponents a peek and see if you can come to an agreement.

2. Be extremely careful not to displace the pallino or bocce balls during measuring. If you do move a ball and cannot agree on its placement, it is good form to award the point to the team not responsible for the illegal movement. Some players like to secure the object ball's position by pressing down on it during measurement. This might be okay for informal play, but no one should touch any balls during measurement. It only increases the chance that you will inadvertently move a ball.

3. To score a point, a ball has to be closer to the pallino than the other team's ball. A tie just doesn't cut it. If, when the frame is completed, you determine that the closest balls rolled by Team A and Team B are tied (equal distance from the pallino), no points are scored. These balls do not cancel each other out and make the next closest ball a point. Again, no points may be scored when the two closest balls are from opposite teams and are equidistant from the object ball.

4. If one, two, or three points are sure, and two opposing team's balls are the next closest to pallino and tied, the previously determined points are scored, but the tied balls mean nothing.

5. Tape measurements (metric units are always preferable to English) are sometimes made from the bocce ball to the center of the pallino (or vice versa). Instruct one person to place the end of the tape measure at the middle (equator) of the bocce ball, and direct another to extend the tape over the top center of the pallino and to read the result. This method requires a little estimation on the part of the measurer in terms of interpreting just where the center of the pallino is. The method is adequate, but can cause problems when two measurements are very close. Some players prefer to measure from the outer dimensions of the balls, but the best and most accurate way to determine which ball is in is with *inside measure*. You want to know which ball has the smaller amount of space between it and the pallino. Hold the tape measure or other device in between the two balls, measuring from the middle (equator) of one to the middle of the other (see photo next page). Then move to the other ball in contention and compare your two findings.

Utilizing a tape measure to determine point

Experienced players can call very close points "by eye". Standing by the object ball, they get a vantage point allowing them to gauge the relative positions of the balls in question. I've consistently been on the losing end of matches with Wonderful World Of Bocce Association president Rico Daniele of Springfield, Massachusetts (www.playbocce.com). It not only amazes me how good a player he is, but also how he can call "eyeball" a point that is "in" by a mere fraction of an inch.

One player handling a measurement alone

Example of inside measure

Play Ball!

Now you know enough to play. Give it a shot and come back and read some more later. In some rounds you may have difficulty telling which ball is closest to the object ball. Remember to get the best angle for determining which ball is in by standing by the object ball. If you cannot make the call by eye, you will have to resort to measurement. In subsequent chapters, we'll take you deeper into the strategy and finer points of play. For now, you know enough to go out and enjoy this great and ancient game.

The Romans played with somewhat rounded stones 2000 years ago. You can play with an inexpensive set of bocce balls or even your candlepin or duckpin bowling balls (just to try out the game). Trent Formaggioni of Springfield, Massachusetts told me that as a child he played with eight softballs and a golf ball or baseball. "We used markers to differentiate each team's softballs, and we played on the grass at our neighborhood park." As an adult he competed in the World Cup of Bocce held in the Imperial Ballroom of Atlantic City's Trump Plaza. "I love the game - on both levels!" he proclaims with joy.

Dozen Steps To The Joy of Bocce

1.   Secure a set of bocce balls, a place to play, and some players.

2.   Make two equal teams. One-, two- or four-person teams are most common.

3.   Toss a coin or otherwise select who will play first.

4.   The team that wins the coin toss pitches the pallino and then rolls the first bocce ball, trying to draw as near as possible to the pallino.

5.   The starting team stands aside and does not bowl again until the opposing team gets one of their bocce balls closer to the pallino or runs out of bocce balls.

6.   Play proceeds in this manner, observing the nearest ball rule. The team with the nearest ball stands aside and waits until such time that the other team has the nearest ball or has used up all its balls in the attempt. Remember – the team that is out *plays* – the team that is in *delays*.

7.   After both teams deliver all balls, the frame or round is over. Score one point for each ball that is closer to the pallino than the closest ball of your opponent.

8.   The team that scores the point(s) starts the next frame by rolling the pallino and the first bocce ball.

9.   Games can be played to 11, 12, 15, 16, 21 points, or to any mutually agreeable count. North American Open Rules call for games of at least 12 points.

10.   Balls can be tossed underhand or overhand, through the air or bowled along the ground.

11.   Think ahead – like chess. Possible strategies include knocking an opponent's ball out of scoring position, redirecting the pallino to a new position, and leaving a ball in front of the pallino to block your opponent's attempt.

12.   Have fun with this wonderful and ancient pastime – the best kept secret in sports.

Play on a ball field

Play on a level patch of grass

Play on hilly terrain

Play at the beach

Play in the snow

Play on a court

Chapter 3
The Terminology

It helps to know what you are talking about

The terms that follow are listed alphabetically. Rather than a technical glossary, this section is designed in an easy-to-read format. It will familiarize the reader with words and situations that are used throughout the rest of the text. A brief perusal of these will set the stage for a clearer understanding of the chapters that follow. From *bank shot* to *winning score*, this sampling of bocce jargon will get you rolling in the right direction. Keep in mind that there is a difference between the way the game is played in recreational and tournament settings and the way it is played in international competition.

bank shot – when playing on courts complete with side and backboards, a shot caromed off the side and/or backboard (illegal in international play).

sequence of a bank shot

33

bocce – sometimes spelled bocci or boccie – can refer to the balls used in the game or the game itself (e.g. players roll their bocce balls while enjoying a game of bocce). The balls can be made of wood, plastic, or composite material. Each of the eight balls in a set is four to five inches in diameter and weighs about two pounds. One team's

A set of bocce balls

balls are distinguished from another's by color (e.g. four green balls, four red balls, and a smaller object ball or pallino of another color). In some sets, balls of the same color are inscribed with distinctive engraving so that teammates' balls can be differentiated from each other. In international volo play the balls are metallic (often an alloy like bronze). Note: As stated earlier, the word bocce means the game and the implement used to play the game (much like baseball refers to the ball and the game). Purists don't refer to the game as bocce ball. It is improper to ask "Do you want to play bocce ball?" or "Are you entered in the bocce ball tournament?" This would be like going to the ice rink and asking if anyone wanted to play hockey puck. "Do you want to play bocce?" and "Are you entered in the bocce tournament?" represent accepted usage. The word is also properly used in this manner: "Roll your bocce off the sideboard."

Dr. Angelo Cordano, one of the top Italian-American players, gives us this lesson to clarify the Italian...

"**Boccia** is a single ball (UNA / ONE ball)

Boccie is the PLURAL - i.e. six boccie

and **Bocce** is the GAME we like."

bocce court or **bocce alley** (sometimes called the **campo**, occasionally **pit**, but this is more properly used for horseshoes) – the enclosed playing surface complete with side and endboards. The surface may be a fine gravel, clay, stone dust, crushed limestone, or oyster flour. Occasionally, court surfaces are grass, indoor/outdoor carpet or other artificial material. Courts are generally 60 to 90 feet in length (90 feet for international competition). Sixty-foot courts (common in the east) are a tad short for serious players. Seventy to 76 feet seems to be a fair compromise between 60' and 90'. Ten to 12 feet in width is acceptable. Sideboards should be at least as high as the balls (8 to 12 inches recommended) and higher at both ends where high velocity shots are more likely to knock the pallino out of the playing area. The United States Bocce Federation strongly recommends 90 feet in length by 13 feet in width. These dimensions provide a court suitable for international rules as well as for open recreational rules. See Chapter 8, Building a Backyard Court, for more details on court dimensions and construction.

bocce courts

boules – the French word for the balls and their version of the game – also called pétanque. The balls are metallic and much smaller and lighter than bocce balls. The object ball (*but* or *cochonnet*) is significantly smaller, too (on the order of a table tennis ball). The game of boules is played on dirt or gravel without side or endboards. It is difficult to play on grass because even closely cropped lawns are likely to obscure the tiny object ball. The game is very similar to bocce and it is not much of a stretch to accept that bocce, boules, and lawn bowling all had a common ancestor.

bowls – the English game of lawn bowling and the balls themselves. The balls are biased (weighted on one side) so hook shots are prevalent. The name bocce is sometimes used interchangeably with lawn bowling but, despite their similarities, they are two different games.

court markings – when playing on an enclosed court, as opposed to a patch of grass or dirt, the court has lines as prescribed by rule (regulations may vary from area to area). For this discussion, let's assume a 76-foot court. To begin a frame, the pallino must cross the half court mark which is 38' from the end. A pallino toss short of this line must be picked up and rolled again. Some rules mandate a line at each end of the court four feet from the back or endboard across which the pallino may not pass on the initial toss. In other words, the playable area for the first toss of pallino is beyond the 38-foot mark and before the 72-foot line. While play progresses, the position of the pallino may change by being hit by another ball (intentionally or accidentally). It may come to rest beyond the 72-foot line, but it may never end up closer to the players than midcourt, or the frame is dead and must be played over. (In addition, some rules call for the pallino to come to rest a minimum of 12 inches from the side boards.)

dead ball – a disqualified ball. In outdoor, recreational bocce using "open rules," there is almost never a dead ball. In club and tournament play on enclosed courts, a ball may be disqualified if:

•there is a penalty such as a foot foul
•it leaves the court's playing surface
•it comes into contact with a person or object which is outside the court

•it hits the top of the court boards
•it hits the covering of the courts or any supports

doubles – the game of bocce played with partners (two against two). Each player rolls two balls.

end – see **frame** below.

endboards – on a court, the backboards at each end. Players often carom shots off the side and endboards attempting to score points although international rules prohibit play off the side and endboards. Rather than just a static backboard, most courts have an additional swinging or hanging board that serves to absorb the force of a hard shot and prevent a long rebound. The facing of these swinging boards is often covered with an absorbent material (old fire hose, rubber tubing, etc.). On long shots, this prevents a player from getting close to the pallino simply by smacking the endboard and relying on the rebound effect to bring the ball into scoring position. Rather, a more skillful shot involving smooth touch and release is required.

foul line – on enclosed courts the line the player must stand behind when rolling his bocce ball. Many players move forward

Sometimes foul lines are marked on the sideboards

as they release the ball, using a three- or four-step delivery as in tenpin bowling. The ball must be released before the player passes the foul line. Some rules specify two foul lines – especially for play on shorter courts. For example, many 60-foot courts have a pointing line four feet from each end and a shooting or hitting line nine feet from each end. Many players take several steps in their approach when trying to hit a ball away. This would not be possible without a longer runway to work with. On the other hand, this longer runway would bring the player too close to his target while attempting to close in for a point, so he would have to deliver his ball from behind the four-foot line when pointing. Some groups who play on longer courts approve one foul line for both pointing and hitting, reasoning that the greater distance makes the pointing line unnecessary.

fouls – (also foot fouls, foot line fouls) – violations of the rules caused by a player stepping over the pointing line or hitting line before the ball leaves the player's hand. Players may not step over the foremost part of the line with any part of the foot before the ball leaves the hand. Some sets of rules call for one warning on a foot foul. Subsequent fouls carry penalties.

frame – also end or round; The period of time during which players from both teams roll their bocce balls from one end of the court to the other and points are awarded – similar to an inning in baseball or softball. When points are tallied, the frame is completed. If a Team A scores one point each frame and the winning score is twelve, the contest will last twelve frames. Unlike softball or baseball, with games of seven or seven innings, the number of frames played in bocce is not predetermined.

hitting – (see also **raffa**) – Rolling the ball with great force to displace a ball or balls, also shooting, spocking, popping, bombing. Since players often use a two-, three-, or four-step delivery for this shot, they may advance to the second foul line (hitting or spocking line) for this shot (assuming the court uses separate lines for pointing and hitting). The ball must be released before the foot crosses the foul line. Some rules define a hit attempt as a throw with speed sufficient enough that it would hit the backboard if it missed its target. This is not always a satisfactory definition since, with fast, hard-packed court surfaces, it doesn't take a forceful roll for a ball to reach the backboard. In other words, a missed point attempt may hit the endboard and, by the letter of the law, it would be a hit attempt.

initial point – the first ball thrown toward the object ball becomes the "in" ball and establishes the initial point. It is always incumbent on the team with pallino advantage to establish the initial point.

in – closest to the pallino. "Our team's ball is 'in' so your team must play the next ball." Some say "This red ball is *holding* the point."

lag – also pointing; to roll for point. To deliver the bocce ball as close to the pallino as possible.

live ball – any ball that has a possibility of scoring a point. Any legally played ball that is resting on the court or in motion as the result of being hit by another live ball. Also, any ball still in the possession of a participant waiting to play.

measuring devices – feet, hands, fingers, twigs, string, tape measures, television antennas, or more specialized implements for determining who has the point. See Chapter 2, The Game, for details on measuring and Chapter 6, The Equipment, for information on purchasing the devices.

nearest ball rule – accepted order of play whereby the team with the ball nearest to the object ball stands aside and allows the other team to bowl until they establish the nearest ball (or they run out of balls in the attempt). The obligation to deliver the next ball always belongs to the team that is "out", not "in". The same team may roll two, three, even four balls in succession if they cannot outlag or knock away the other team's point while attempting to establish the "in" ball.

open rules – a less structured type of play unencumbered by the stringent regulations of international play. Open rules usually govern backyard play as well as a good deal of league and tournament competition. See Chapter 11, Tournament Play & Rules.

out – not closest to the pallino. "Your team's ball is in. Our team's ball is out, so it's our turn to roll."

pallino – also called the pallina, object ball, jack, pill, cue ball. A ball that is smaller than the bocce balls (generally 1 3/8 inches in diameter as opposed to 4 ¼ inches for the larger bocce balls) that is the target in the game of bocce. In a true contest of one-up-manship, teams vie to score points by directing their balls closer to this ball than the opposition can. The pallino, bocce's bull's eye, is always of a color visibly distinct from both teams' bocce balls.

pallino advantage – the favorable position of possessing control of the object ball. The team with pallino advantage gets to roll the pallino to any legal position and must also play the first bocce ball in the round. Pallino advantage is established at the beginning of the game by coin toss (or choosing up, or some other mutually agreeable method) and subsequently goes in each round to the team that scores.

pétanque – see **boules** above

pointing – also lagging; rolling the bocce ball in an effort to "close in" or draw near the pallino. This is a finesse shot requiring deft touch and smooth release of the ball. It is an attempt to get as close as possible to the object ball – to score a point. Sometimes this is referred to as the punto or puntata (gentle) method. If there are separate foul lines for pointing and hitting, players must use the pointing or roll line (the one closer to the end from which you are playing) for this shot. Those skilled at pointing are considered good pointers or laggers. During a postgame recap you may reflect that your team pointed very well but your shooting was off.

punto – smooth roll for point. See **pointing**.

raffa – (see also **hitting**) – a fast rolling shot intended to knock an opponent's ball away or to drive the pallino to a new position. Striking its target on the roll, this smash shot is referred to as hitting, spocking, popping, or bombing. Raffa shots usually include a two-, three-, or four-step approach reminiscent of tenpin bowling. Although a raffa in recreational play is usually rolled like a bowler trying for a strike, a true international raffa must be lofted beyond the raffa line, which is three meters in front of the pointing or lagging line.

round – same as frame above.

rule of advantage – the option given to a team when opponents have committed an infraction. The option is to accept the result of the illegal play or to remove the illegally delivered ball and return all displaced balls to their previous positions.

selling the point – colorful expression used when a player inadvertently gives the point to his opponent by 1) knocking his own ball out of contention, 2) bumping the opponent's ball into scoring position or 3) redirecting the pallino away from his team's ball(s) or toward the other team's ball(s). "I'm so angry at myself. I sold the point!"

sideboards – on enclosed rectangular courts, a continuous railing of 10- to 12-inch high wood planking (often pressure treated) that serves to keep bocce balls on the court and in play.

singles – the game of bocce played one-on-one with each player rolling four balls. Sometimes referred to as testa/testa (head to head).

spock – to hit a ball with great force to displace its position. Derived from the Italian spaccare, to break. Americanized, the term is generally used as a verb, "I'll try to spock the ball that's closest to the pallino." Players may advance to the spock line when attempting this shot (also called a hit, pop, or bomb). See **hitting** above.

spock line – also hitting line; on official courts, the line over which a player attempting to hit or spock may not pass until the ball has left the hand.

standing hitter – a player who attempts to hit without taking an approach. Remaining stationary, the player releases a raffa or volo shot. Though they use no approach steps, these players are entitled to advance to the hitting line.

swingboard – see **endboards**.

testa/testa – see **singles** above.

triples – a three versus three bocce match. Each player rolls two balls, so twelve bocce balls are in play.

unified – in Special Olympics, a doubles game pairing Special Olympians and their Special Partners on the same team.

volo – an aerial shot to knock an opponent's ball out of scoring position or displace the pallino. Skilled players need to approach 80 to 90% success rate on these airborne knockaway attempts. Some tournament events hold shoot-outs (like the NBA three-point shoot-out) where players compete in a voloing exhibition. Target balls are placed at different locations on the court, some behind other balls adding to the difficulty, and players try to take the volo title by scoring the greatest number of hits.

winning score – bocce games may be played to any predetermined count. Winning totals of 11, 12, 15, and 16 are most common. Unlike some other sports, you don't have to win by two points. The team to first reach the agreed upon score wins the game.

Random Thoughts On Bocce Jargon

One of the things that fascinates me about bocce is not only the variation of play in pockets across the country, but also the jargon that has evolved in different locations. It bugs me no end when someone asks, "Want to play some bocce ball?" I think of a kid going to the hockey rink or frozen pond and asking his friends if they want to play some "hockey puck." Although American bocce is still struggling to standardize, we should at least agree to call the game "bocce", and reserve "bocce ball" for the round object we roll in the direction of the pallino.

Some refer to the object ball in the masculine (pallino) while others in the feminine (pallina). I also hear jack, kitty, pill, cue ball, mark, and every variation beginning with the letter P from Pauline to piñata.

Hitting an opponent's ball to displace it because it is "in" for a point is one of the nifty skill shots in bocce. If it happens to be a red ball that has the point, I've heard talk about making a shot called a "Visine" – one that's designed to "get the red out!"

And I've heard of closing in for point referred to as "coodling in."
"You have about two feet to work with – coodle right in here for the point."

On the south side of Chicago they "toots it up" when they tap a ball gently to push it closer to the pallino to score the point. A player might counsel his partner with "Roll gently and toots our ball up a little closer to the target." Therefore, this could logically be called a "Tootsie Roll."

Scoring four points in one frame is sometimes referred to as a "four-bagger," like a homerun in baseball. When a team gets all four points in a frame with a neat cluster around the object ball, players from the Long Island Bocce Club call that "four on the floor" or a

43

"casino." To them, pallino advantage is "pallino power" or "power of the pallino". In Massachusetts players talk about "running the rail" for bank shots or rolls that hug the sideboards.

Players from various Massachusetts communities use some colorful terms.

A ball that is "in" is referred to as "holding point."

"This green ball is holding the point right now," a player would advise his teammate.

Hitting a previously played ball a little closer to the pallino is "bucking it up."

"If you can buck this red ball up a couple inches, it will be in."

The term "cover" means two things – get the point, or block the opponents' path to the pallino.

"You only need to get a ball within three feet to cover" (win the point for your team).

"Cover up by leaving a ball right in front" (leave a ball short to block).

Bocce Warfare Terms

Russell Dean Newman, writing for the Chattanooga Times Free Press, learned about bocce a few years ago at the Chattanooga Southeastern Tournament. His view of the "arsenal" of bocce "weapons" is clever and proves him a quick study. I get the feeling he may have been a military brat.

Here are his definitions: (reprinted with permission)…

"The volo - a flying bocce smart bomb with a reverse spin. Goes over, not through, a cluttered field of play. Surprise attack from above removes enemy bocce and establishes allied outpost near pallina. Stops at point of impact. It takes practice, troops, lots of practice."

"The raffa - a smashing shot executed at low altitudes. Targets and removes single opponent. Requires little precision. Acceptable as overhand or underhand release. Knocks out opposing formation around pallina. Often unpredictable results."

Bluff View Arts District, Chattanooga, TN
Site of the Chattanooga Southeastern Tournament

"The puntata - a slow-motion rolling offense. Ground-based. Best used early in play. Requires gentle touch and finesse. Travels straight path on flat terrain. Puts opponents on defensive."

Chapter 4
The Game, A Closer Look ▬▬▬▬▬▬

Now that you have read about and played a little bocce, let's take a closer look at the ancient pastime. When Italian immigrants at the turn of the century landed at Ellis Island, bocce passed through customs with them. Once in America, Italians tended to keep the game to themselves, playing in backyards and at their social clubs. For many, it was a way of hanging on to the old country – a nostalgic glimpse of their native land. From the outset it was an Italian's diversion, and it was distinctively an Italian *man's* sport. Bocce's recent resurgence is largely due to the fact that non-Italians, young players and women have embraced the game. The increasing number of courts constructed in public parks is also promoting the sport's growth. Today, parents who want to share the game with their children don't have to spend the afternoon at the social club. They can get outside and enjoy the game and the outdoors. While Italians still seem to be the most zealous advocates of bocce (and very good players). They now share the fun with others. Anyone can play, regardless of age, strength or physical condition. If you can roll a ball about the size and weight of a candlepin bowling ball, you can play. Bocce has truly become a game for all people. Having moved slowly but steadily away from its ethnic and male dominated upbringing, bocce is reaching the mainstream.

Still, we promoters of this great game have a way to go. Sometimes referred to as the "best kept secret in sports," there is still a segment of the North American population that has no knowledge of the game. Radio talk show hosts continue to ask me "How do you play?" and "What is the object?" And callers to the radio station ask if bocce is similar to shuffleboard, lawn bowls, and boules. Most obvious is that bocce still suffers from an "image problem". People envision cranky old coots smoking cigars and drinking wine while engaged in "geriatric lawn bowling". And the tone of voice and demeanor of the talk show hosts often reveal their sense that bocce is not really to be taken seriously. While talking bocce on CSRB in Toronto (the largest talk radio show in Canada) the sports director chimed in with "Hey Mario, is there any checking in bocce?"

While those of us promoting this wonderful sport still have our work cut out for us, the up side is that virtually everyone we introduce the game to enjoys it.

Quite similar to the French game of boules or pétanque and the English game of lawn bowls, bocce has subtle differences. Pétanque uses small metal balls that are lofted in an underhand, palm down fashion. And while some use the term bocce as a synonym for lawn bowling, the two are different games. Lawn bowls are large, biased balls which curve or hook during their path to the target. In the United States, bocce is much more widely played than lawn bowls and boules. But when grouped together, the three ball-and-target games stand with soccer and golf as the three largest participatory sports in the world.

Bocci Ball

By Frank Cappelli

How 'bout a friendly game of bocci?
We'll take our turns, we'll take our aim so nicely
We'll throw the little round poleena now
Throw the ball

The bocci ball
Please go first and toss your ball as close to the poleena as you can
Throw the ball
The bocci ball
We all watch as you show us how you play the game, mio caro amico
Your toss is smooth, we look and lean-a
The ball is going toward the small poleena
We can see it is a very good toss
Throw the ball
The bocci ball
We have heard you, now we see you, all the best to you, oh mio caro
amico
Your toss is smooth, we look and lean-a
The ball is going toward the small poleena
We can see it is a very good toss
Throw the ball
The bocci ball
Let us watch you as you try to get your ball slightly closer than mine
Your toss is grand, we watch and lean-a
The ball is going toward the small poleena
And we can see it is a very good toss
Throw the ball
The bocci ball
It's your turn and we all see how good at bocci ball you really,
really, really are
Your toss is smooth, we look and lean-a
The ball is going toward the small poleena
We can see it is a very good toss
We walk together toward the small poleena
To find who's closer and to find the winn-a
It's a tie so let us play again

Lyrics reprinted from the musical cassette tape *Pass the Coconut* with permission of F.E. Cappelli Publishing Co., 717 North Meadowcroft Ave., Pittsburg, PA 15216.

Bocce's Attraction Today

Formal bocce is played on courts of hard, compacted clay, stone dust or oyster shell with round, unbiased balls four to five inches in diameter and weighing about two pounds. Singles, doubles, triples, and games with foursomes are popular with very little variation in the rules. Bocce requires good judgment of distance and the ability to size up a situation and determine what type of shot or strategy is called for. An eye for analyzing the contour and rough spots or divots on a playing surface is helpful, too. Some bocce players claim that the game helps their golf, bowling, shuffleboard and horseshoes since it has features of all these games. In one way, the game is like slow-pitch softball. The slow-pitch delivery, with its six- to twelve-foot arc, is easy to hit, but not that easy to hit well. Similarly, bocce is easy to play, but not that easy to play well. "Although an easy game to learn," comments Phil Ferrari, president of the World Bocce Association, "bocce takes a lifetime to master."

Played widely in the United States both as an organized sport and as informal recreation, part of bocce's attraction is that it can be learned in minutes. Another plus for bocce is that the subtle nuances and strategies of play are endless. People learn how to play quickly, since the open rules are easily understood, but they continue learning as long as they compete. Equipment costs are minimal, and maintenance expense is virtually nonexistent, which makes bocce doubly attractive in this era of budgetary restraint. Though there exists a wide range of specialized bocce shoes, clothing and exotic measuring devices, all you really need is a set of bocce balls and a place to play. Youth and physical attributes are not essential, and games lasting 15 minutes to several hours are played indoors and out. The length of games depends on the skill of the competitors and the type of game being played (contests governed by international rules played by very skillful players tend to be long games).

Bocce players come in all ages and both sexes. Increasingly, the physically and mentally challenged are taking part in the game. Finally, there are very few injuries associated with bocce (okay, so you might drop a ball on your toe occasionally). Sometimes a bocce ball or pallino becomes a dangerous projectile made airborne by a volo or raffa shot. Fences around spectator areas are common and are being constructed with fine mesh to contain the pallino (especially near the ends where the greatest number of balls become missiles). It is safest to watch a game from the sides or from the end of the shooter, rather than from the end toward which the balls are rolling.

Many courts are currently located in social clubs requiring paid membership, but a movement is on to bring the game out of the private sector and into the public. To this end, public outdoor courts are being constructed in many parts of the country. In addition, we hear investors talk of building indoor courts and renting playing time as in a pool hall or bowling alley. One such venue is Campo di Bocce in Los Gatos, California (565 University Ave. – telephone: 408-395-7650). A blurb from their web site (www.campodibocce. com) reads "Eight world-class bocce courts amid vine covered arbors and cypress tree shaded seating areas. Enjoy our beautiful outdoor patio where you can dine on fine Italian food, relax with friends and, of course, play a little Bocce."

Campo di Bocce, Los Gatos, CA

In the Detroit area the Palazzo di Bocce features 10 indoor courts and an Italian restaurant (palazzodibocce.com). Billed as "America's first palace of bocce," The Palazzo di Bocce is the brainchild of Michigan businessman Anthony Battaglia.

Promotional copy for the Bocce Palace reads…

"Take the court, claim the game that millions enjoy! The debut of Palazzo di Bocce in Orion Township, Michigan, north of Detroit, heralds a new era for the dynamic sport of bocce. This spectacular venue is the first in the U.S. to offer ten bocce courts accessible year-round, in a unique indoor recreational sports and dining facility. Any time is a good time to play bocce. Hearty fun, camaraderie and friendly competition make playing bocce a physically and mentally healthy pursuit. You'll fall in love with this game as you face its athletic and strategic challenges in a cordial and welcoming atmosphere. Be one of the millions of enthusiasts around the world who have rediscovered the compelling game of bocce. It's your court….benvenuto!"

Campo di Bocce and the Palazzo di Bocce are ideal for corporations of all sizes to rent for company outings and parties. They also host league play as well as bocce events for youth, singles, couples, seniors, and others who want to experience the joy and camaraderie of bocce.

Recreational Bocce

Just as Italians brought different dialects to this country – so did they bring regionalized variations of the rules of bocce. A movement toward standardization is gaining momentum, but there is as yet little consistency in the rules of play from one area of the country to another. In Chapter 2 we introduced the game and what have been called open rules, a recreational style of play with very few regulations. The game can proceed unencumbered by endless restrictions for almost anything goes (more on rules in Chapter 11, Tournament Play & Rules).

As we have stated, the game can be played almost anywhere on a variety of surfaces; the backyard, a dirt road, the beach, a golf course, fair grounds or public park. Played on a reasonably level or somewhat hilly surface, the game calls for a variety of skills and strategies and produces rich variations. No two games are ever exactly alike.

The Bocce Shots – Punto, Raffa, & Volo

The playing surface and the position of previously played balls determine which type of delivery is called for. Balls may be rolled gently for point (the punto shot), rolled fast to knock another ball away (the raffa shot), or lofted in the air (volo). For all bocce shots, the ball must be released before the player oversteps the foul line.

The Punto Shot – Pointing

On smooth, fast surfaces, players tend to roll the ball for point, holding it with palm up or palm down. Players with very good touch like to release smoothly, palm up, letting the ball roll off the fingertips. Executed properly, this imparts a 12 o'clock to 6 o'clock rotation on the ball. This release is much like that of a pure shooter in basketball. The hooper follows through with arm extended high, rolling the ball off the fingertips, and sends the ball sailing toward the basket with good backspin.

A good way to practice this fingertip-release bocce delivery is adapted from an old baseball camp throwing drill. Most young ballplayers' throws miss their targets because of poor grip and/or throwing technique. We place a piece of electrical tape around a baseball and have the camper place his middle finger on the stripe and his next fingers to the left and right, with the thumb catching the stripe at the bottom. The baby finger is on the side of the ball. Next, the players enjoy a game of catch, and carefully watch the flight of the ball. With proper grip and throwing motion, the stripe will not wobble as the ball sails to its target.

Wrapping a single piece of electrical tape around the center of a bocce ball, grasp it palm up, with the tape running north to south. Use the grip above (place the middle finger on the tape and one finger on each side of the tape). Since you are rolling with an underhand delivery and the ball is larger, the thumb ends up nearer the top of the ball and not reaching the tape. The little finger rests on the side of the ball for balance, and the roll is executed smoothly off the fingers. Pay close attention to the tape as the ball moves along its path. Thrown properly, the ball reveals a solid black stripe, top to

Taping a ball is an excellent way to
practice pointing

bottom. Any deviation in the stripe or wobbling motion indicates a faulty release (ball coming off the side of the fingers or not coming off fingers evenly).

Many good players roll for point in an entirely different manner. They grip the ball lightly (palm up or down) and toss it a few feet in front of the foul line, releasing all five fingers at once. For them, the touch is in the back swing and release. In either case a good deal of practice is needed to develop the deft release necessary for this most crucial shot in bocce. As we have seen, the game involves strategy, skill and finesse. But, above all, bocce is a game of touch.

Pointing styles

Some Points On Pointing

The grip should be light with the palm facing the target. An alternate style is to face the back of the hand to the target. This release helps slow the ball down on fast courts due to backspin, but makes rolling the ball off the fingertips impossible. Proponents of the palm-down toss maintain that it keeps the ball on line better because the backspin tends to "dig in," preventing the ball from diverting left or right. They also feel that there is less chance for the wrist or hand to twist inadvertently during the delivery since this is a more natural position. If you let your hands hang down by your side, you will see that the palm-up release requires an almost 180-degree rotation of the forearm. Try both types of delivery. See what works best for you. The arm should be kept close to the body during the back swing. The right-hander generally places the left foot forward and the lefty has the right foot forward, but this is not a hard and fast rule. Regardless, most of the body weight should be on the front foot, with the back foot on the ground for balance.

Some players place one foot beside the other, and simply bend at the waist and roll. Still others start with both feet together, then deliver while taking a step forward with one foot. Of course, this makes it necessary for the player to begin a step behind the foul line, while the previous methods allow you to cozy right up to it. Some players move forward over the foul line after the ball is released, maintaining that moving directly toward the target promotes better accuracy. Indeed, in recreational play it is not uncommon to see an enthusiastic player toss his ball and run up behind and then alongside it, encouraging and coaxing it toward its destination.

It is important to bend at the waist and keep the body square to the target. Maintain balance and keep the ball and hand at about the same level as the ankle. Keep the arm path straight throughout the delivery, and make a smooth follow-through. The amount of back swing is directly proportional to the distance the ball must travel.

You may sight directly on the target or pick a spot out in front of the release point as some tenpin bowlers do. "Spot bowlers" claim that it is much easier to hit a closer target. Selecting a target zone or drop zone instead of zeroing in on the object ball is a technique that is controversial among bocce players. Some swear by it. Others swear at it. The first group points out that golfers look at the ball, not the hole when putting and that top notch bowlers key on spots on the lane, not the pins. The other group says it's tough to hit what you're not looking at. Give both styles a go, and decide for yourself. Keeping the head down and focusing on the target (target ball or drop zone) even after releasing the ball fosters good concentration. Experiment with all the deliveries and discover what works best for you. Be advised that most of the top players in the world use the drop zone technique.

Ken Dothee, former president of the United States Bocce Federation, reminds us that the arm and hand are on the side of the body, while the eyes are in the center. "Line up your arm with the target, not the center of your body," says Dothee. "This allows you to make a straight release and prevents the arm from crossing in front of your body during the delivery."

Suggestions For Practicing Pointing

To improve accuracy, here is a technique long used by those learning to become fast-pitch softball pitchers. The would-be pitchers first learn the proper grip and delivery, then find a wall to toss against. Initially, they just try to hit the wall anywhere, and field the carom. With success, they move to increasingly smaller targets, trying to hit inside a large chalked box, then a smaller box, and finally a square approximating the size of the strike zone. Bocce's version of this technique involves marking a large circle on your playing surface. Now roll bocce balls with the right amount of force to get them to stop within the ring. As you gain proficiency, make the circle increasingly smaller. If you roll eight balls, it is not enough to land two or three dead center and scatter the rest outside the circle. To develop consistency is to cluster a majority of the balls somewhere in the target zone every time. When you get to this point, shrink the target. It is important to spend enough time developing a high percentage of accuracy with large circles before progressing to smaller ones. Also, decrease the size of the circle by small increments rather than going directly from a large circumference to a small one.

To hone the ability to roll the ball the proper distance, mark two parallel lines across the court and practice rolling balls that come to rest anywhere within these lines. Vary the position of the parallel lines and practice, practice, practice. This drill and the previous one are more enjoyable if practiced with a partner, adding an element of competition to the activity.

To work on controlling the direction or glide path of the bocce ball, create one-foot wide lanes down the court using cones or other marking devices. Roll the ball evenly at different speeds and practice this very important phase of the game. On a level surface, your goal is to roll each ball from one end to the other without dislodging any cones.

Practicing with cones

To Step Or Not To Step When Pointing

We've discussed different styles of release (I prefer the 12 o'clock to 6 o'clock rotation as the ball rolls off the fingertips). I relate it to basketball. The roundball rolls off the fingertips of the best shooters. It sails to the +hoop with pronounced backspin. If you shoot hoops with a kind of knuckleball release, you can learn to be a pretty good shooter. But you'll never become a truly great shooter. It's the fingertip roll that creates the feathery smooth touch of basketball's "pure shooters."

The next technique to address is whether to step forward as you release, or to plant the feet and move only the arm. I've seen excellent pointers utilizing both styles. The following is from the point of view of a right-hander (lefties just reverse things).

Many of the top players cozy right up to the foul line and place their left foot near the chalk mark. Their right foot is well back toward the backboard for balance. The only motion then, comes from the arm. The arm swings back and forth like a pendulum, and the release is on the forward pass. They like the fact that there is no extraneous body motion. Top players, it seems, reach out and roll the ball well out in front of the body.

The alternate release involves taking what has been called a "glide step." A right-hander would take his position a step behind the foul line with feet together. S/he would step with the left foot and release the ball all in one smooth motion. This, proponents say, gets the entire body involved, rather than just the arm, wrist, and hand. Keep the following four S's in mind. The delivery must be Slow, Smooth, and Steady, with the step Straight toward the target.

It is interesting to note that even high level players have quite varied pointing styles. Some step forward as they roll, some plant their feet. Some deliver from directly in front of the body, while others release slightly to the side.

"There is only one rule in pointing" declares journeyman bocce star Dr. Angel Cordano. "Leave the ball in front of the pallino."

The Raffa

The raffa is a fast rolling shot intending to knock an opponent's ball away or to direct the pallino to a new position. For example, your opponent has pallino advantage and rolls the first ball one inch from the object ball. It's probably going to be easier for you to hit that ball away than to roll one closer than an inch from pallino. Some bocce enthusiasts fear that the raffa's increasing popularity will discourage coed play since women's leagues tend to emphasize finesse and strategy over brute strength, but increasingly women players are employing the various hitting techniques. Donna Allen of the USBF maintains that "The key to the successful raffa shot is the follow-through. Therefore, it has been embraced by women over the more physically demanding volo shot." The result is that women, according to Allen, "are becoming more well-rounded and competitive players."

Reminiscent of a break shot in billiards, the raffa is usually made with an approach similar to that of a tenpin bowler. Remember, on all shots the player must release the ball before overstepping the foul line or a foot foul results. Some sets of rules mandate one foul line for pointing and a second for raffa and volo attempts. This second line, farther up the court, allows the bocce player room for several approach steps. Many players intentionally go over the foul line after releasing the ball. Rather than stopping abruptly at the foul stripe, they prefer to improve accuracy by keeping their body's momentum moving in the direction of the target. Other players take a three- or four-step delivery like in bowling, but stop at the foul line. Still others are standing hitters. They stand still, swinging only the arm, hand, and ball to unload a direct hit on the target. Be aware that on some courts the foul lines are painted on the sideboards while on others they are drawn across the surface of the court. In most informal bocce, many players overstep the foul line before releasing the ball and, though this provokes a good deal of grumbling from opponents, foot fouls are rarely called.

Raffa Technique

As in bowling, players can set their own style of stance, approach and delivery. Rolling a bocce or bowling ball presents fewer absolutes than hitting a baseball or serving a tennis ball. The key is to stay relaxed and comfortable. Some players begin by holding the ball at eye level and sighting over it. Others bend deeply at the waist, and still others hold the ball out at arm's length pointing toward the target. You can choose any style. The important thing is to use the exact same stance, approach and delivery every time. You must develop consistency in front of the foul line before you'll see consistent results down by the object ball.

Your initial distance from the foul line depends on the number and size of the steps in your approach (usually three or four). The feet are together or one is slightly ahead of the other. Keep the body square to the foul line, and practice until your steps are the same length each time. The steps should be straight (watch out for drifting left or right), slow and under control. The raffa attempt on a bocce court requires the same approach as a strike or spare attempt on the bowling alley, without the slide. If you use a three- or four-step (or five-step) approach at the bowling alley, use the same technique during raffa attempts.

In the three-step approach, the ball drops down and back for the back swing during the first step, which the right-hander takes with the left foot. On the second step the ball is almost at the top of the back swing. The third step is the slide in bowling, with shoulders square to the target and the other arm out for balance. Instead of the slide, the bocce player either stops abruptly upon release, or continues across the foul line *after the release* (top players continue forward after the release). The four-step approach is similar to the three-step approach with the additional step beginning with the right foot (for right-handers). Many players need this extra step to bring the entire stance, approach and delivery into synch. Regardless of the number of steps, they must be natural, rhythmic and well-coordinated.

The raffa technique - in international play a true raffa must be lofted beyond the raffa line which is three meters in front of the pointing line

Speed Versus Accuracy

There are many hard hitters in bocce, often an example of overkill. A direct hit with high velocity sends the target ball flying, but often results in a long post-impact roll for the raffa. You've displaced the opponent's close point, but your ball isn't very near to the pallino either. Of course, if you had a previously played ball(s) close to the pallino, a clean takeout of the opponent's ball brings it (them) into scoring position. If you are determined to become a hard thrower, make sure that you do not sacrifice accuracy for speed.

Key Points To Emphasize For The Raffa

1. Bend at the waist during the approach and delivery.
2. Keep the arm swing close to the body.

3. The back swing should not be higher than shoulder level.

4. Make the approach steps in a straight line to the target.

5. The first step should be taken by the foot opposite to the throwing arm.

6. Keep the shoulders square to the target.

7. Release the ball on the last step with knees and toes pointing straight at the target.

8. Do not release too soon. Bend at the waist and extend and extend the arm, letting go of the ball out in front of the body (but toward the side of the throwing hand eye).

9. If you prefer rolling off the fingertips, roll the ball like a bowler trying for a strike. If you prefer the loft or lob, then the farther the target the higher your release point should be. Proponents of this method claim that the farther the ball rolls, the more its chance of going off line.

10. Follow through high with a full sweep of the arm.

11. Stress accuracy over speed.

12. Keep the arm path in a straight pendulum-type swing – the arm goes down, back, forward, and to follow-through position in the same constant arc.

13. Make the elements of the stance, approach, delivery and follow-through consistent every time.

14. Emphasize concentration, which is a critical factor in increasing the percentage of hits.

Some Suggestions For Practicing Raffa

Spend some time working on stance, approach and delivery with no ball. Start by assuming a comfortable starting point and stance, and walk up to the foul line concentrating on just the steps (no arm movement). Next, walk the approach and add the arm swing, delivering an imaginary ball. Now pick up the ball and go through the motion again, but do not roll the ball. Let the weight of the ball do the work of the arm swing. Finally, make a complete approach and delivery rolling at a target. Place target balls at close range for practice until you can hit 80% or better. Then move the target farther away. Remember to make the approach to the launch point slow and smooth and at a constant speed. Fouling often occurs when steps are too long or too fast. Have someone watch you for foot fouls or set up a video camera perpendicular to the foul line. If you have difficulty hitting your target even at close range, try making the target larger by placing several balls in a cluster. As your percentage of hits increases, make the target increasingly smaller, then increasingly farther away. Practice, practice, practice.

Most of the recreational players I meet and play with have the same "flaw" in their game. They can point pretty well, but are weak at hitting. I hear a lot of "Well, I'm not very good at that, so I'll try to close in instead." To be a complete player you must be adept at all facets of the game. Major league baseball teams look for the "multi-tooled player" - the one who can throw, run, field, hit for average, and hit for power. Top flight bocce calls for the deft touch of pointing, the skillful precision of hitting, and the cerebral aspect that tells us when to do which. The first step for recreational players is to go ahead and try to hit when the situation warrants it. You won't get any better at hitting by avoiding it. Consider this...a very shrewd basketball coach once told me that, "A good shooter is a bad shooter who kept shooting." Keep hitting.

Start practicing by putting your target fairly close and don't move it back until you can consistently hit it at that short range. You decide what consistency level is right for you (70%, 80%, greater, less?). If your goal is 90% hitting accuracy, don't move the target back until you can hit it 9 times out of 10. Good basketball free throw shooters sometimes end practice by making ten foul shots in a row. You might think that ten straight is not so many for a skilled player, but the shooter in this drill counts only swishes. Balls that go in, after first hitting the backboard, rim or flange don't count ("nothing but net" is the goal). Adapt this strategy to your hitting practice so that hits only count if they drive the target toward the backboard. Any glancing blow that sends the target veering to the left or right doesn't count. For even more challenging accuracy, use the pallino as target rather than a bocce ball. Having a practice partner at the other end makes efficient use of time. S/he practices hitting back toward your end, conveniently returning the balls for your next set.

Note: In international play, a raffa may not be rolled all the way to its target. There are court lines at points A, B, and C. Your release for a raffa is at point B, but the ball must pass point C before it strikes the ground (see Chapter 12 – International Play).

The Volo

Note: The suggestions listed here apply to the volo shot in backyard or recreational settings. True international volo shots must meet certain additional restrictions. See Chapter 12, International Play. {I love the volo shot, although I'm not very good at it. Many open rules tournaments outlaw the volo because of insurance liability, and others disallow the shot on short courts figuring that it is too easy to hit close targets}

When playing on grass, rough, or soft surfaces, it is often necessary to loft the ball into the air, letting it bounce and then run up to the target. This is a form of what bocce players call a volo shot (an aerial toss). The volo, traditionally used to knock an opponent's ball away, allows for better accuracy than rolling on rough, uneven surfaces. With practice altering the height and distance of the lob and analyzing the subsequent roll of the ball, a player can add this effective weapon to his arsenal of shots.

Some players loft the ball half way or more toward the target and let it run the rest of the way. The volo shot is best controlled by holding the ball palm down. Sometimes you will need to throw it with backspin to get it to stop quickly after it lands. For very long volos, you may want to toss the ball with the palm facing up to impart more forward spin thus increasing its post-landing carry. In any case, unless your lawn is very level, it is often difficult to roll for points on grass with consistent results.

A variation of this shot is good for dealing with rough surface just in front of the playing line. Simply lob the ball over the rough area and let it roll to the target. For a short lob, release the ball at about the level of the knee. The faster the surface, the higher the release point and trajectory. For high loft shots, the release point should be at the level of the upper thigh or above. The longer the toss, the more exaggerated the back swing must be. Swing the arm in a straight line with the target and push off the legs on the release. Follow through high. Practice by placing an object on the playing surface over which the ball must pass on its way to the target.

The traditional volo shot is tossed into the air in an attempt to strike its target on the fly. A skillful player can make a neat transfer of energy shot in which his ball hits the opponent's ball, sending it flying but leaving his ball in the approximate spot that it struck. Another option is to strike the ground with the volo a foot or two before the target, and have it hit the target on the roll. After the initial impact, the volo's energy of motion is transferred to the target ball which ricochets away leaving your ball in contention. However, depending on the type of surface and the kind of ball used, a short volo can bounce right over its target.

Top bocce players use an approach similar to the raffa approach when delivering a volo. However, the stance and approach are much more upright and the ball is usually tossed with palm down. Most volo shooters use a four-step approach and continue moving past the foul line directly toward the target after they release the ball. We suggest mastering the stationary throw before progressing to this technique.

Volo Technique

Begin working on the last two steps of the four-step approach since these are the most critical. During these steps the arm swing and launch is made. Breaking down and mastering these two steps, then, is essential before advancing.

Stand at the foul line with feet together and arms by the side. Take two steps backward to bring yourself into correct position for this drill. The first step is taken with the foot opposite the throwing arm. As this step is taken, bring the arm swing back in a straight pendulum-like movement. The arm should be at the top of the back swing as the second step is started. The arm comes forward to the launch point on the second step. Continue to move forward toward the target after you release the ball. This follow-through fosters better accuracy, and is not a foot foul unless you overstep the line before releasing the shot.

Two-step approach

Once the two-step approach is mastered, advance to the four-step method. Begin four steps from the foul line with feet together and arms by the side. Many players prefer a stance with the ball held at waist, chest or eye level. With this stance the ball is often held palm up and rotated into palm down position during the arm swing. Again, the first step should be with the foot opposite to the throwing hand. The arm does not begin the back swing on this step. The back swing begins on the second step and should not reach the top of its arc until the end of the third step. The fourth step brings the arm forward in a straight line with the target and the ball is released. During the follow-through phase, the voloist continues moving in a straight line to the target, promoting greater accuracy. Use the same suggestions for practicing raffa shots listed previously for honing your volo skills. Using two sets of bocce balls when working on the volo and raffa shots makes for a more efficient practice session (more repetitions before walking to the other end of the play area to "reload"). Another option is to practice with a partner stationed at the other end. You shoot at targets at his end and he returns the balls to your end with his practice shots.

Four-step approach

Basketball guru Dave DeVenzio describes in his book, *Smart Moves*, how he went to the playground early in the morning before high school to practice his game. His goal was to become the best high school basketball player in the nation, in part, by out-practicing the competition. "The extra hours of practice I was getting were not nearly as important as the confidence I was developing. Nearly everyone with whom I was competing was sleeping while I was advancing, getting better." DeVenzio was named the best high school basketball player in Pennsylvania and one of the top five players in the nation. So, I want everybody reading this to develop the bocce confidence you need by getting up at 5:00 AM every day to practice.

Compete At Your Own Level

With bocce's flexibility and simplicity there is a style and level of play for you. But we must warn you. The game grows on you and eventually you'll yearn to play at the next higher level. You start out playing on the backyard lawn and long for a court. You play on the court and you want to join a league or participate in tournaments. It is inevitable. Don't fight it. The beauty of the game is that it can be enjoyed on so many different levels – from recreational play in your backyard on grass, dirt, or gravel to more structured play at the social club or outdoor courts. For some, tournament play involving singles, doubles, triples, or four-person teams is the way to go. And tournament play ranges from the very low key to the extremely cutthroat (see Chapter 11, Tournament Play & Rules). Bocce players can even compete at the national and international level, representing their country in world championship tournaments. And the International Olympics Committee has recognized bocce as a sport. This is the important first step toward its becoming an Olympic sport.

Bocce is about to explode in this country. LL Bean's summer catalog advertises bocce balls in a handsome carrying case and, yes, designer bocce shoes are in vogue. "Bocce," said one thirty-something couple, "is the yuppiest thing we do." Bocce's small but enthusiastic band of promoters expects it to become one of the top recreational sports in the USA. A set of bocce balls will be as common a household item as a television set. Experiencing ever-rising popularity, indoor bocce courts are sprouting up in restaurants, lounges and sports bars in various parts of the country. You can play some friendly bocce while waiting to be served, and settle the bill over a game afterward.

The introduction of bocce in American schools is beginning to gain momentum, with young people taking to the game readily. In Wilbraham, Massachusetts, bocce buff Leonard Hickey built a

High schoolers enjoying Len Hickey's court
in Wilbraham, Massachusetts

gorgeous 76-foot long court on his business property. He installed spectator benches, and lights the court from dusk to dawn. Local high school students spend some evenings there and are proving to be naturals at the sport. They understand the game immediately and are rapidly developing their own bocce jargon.

"You scored the point, so you get pallino privilege – it's like having the honors in golf."

"That ball is too close to beat, so take it out!"

"Yea, it's near the sideboard, so run the rail and take 'em out!"

"Good idea, even if you miss, we have three pellets left."

Maria Colangelo, a teacher of Italian at Plainville High in Connecticut runs a bocce week that culminates with a popular bocce tournament. The tourney is open only to students in her classes, a strategy that has boosted course enrollment over the years. The students practice bocce on the lawns on campus, then play at a local Italian club where the members serve as referees. The players are permitted to speak only Italian when asking questions of the referee, and of course, the official can only respond via the romance language. Ms. Colangelo's excellent program is well covered by local media, and is typical of the response bocce will get in schools in the future.

It is amazing that within such a simple and elegant framework of play, bocce provides such limitless variation. From backyard lawns to international competitions, bocce is truly a game for all people. And in what other arena could an 80-year-old grandparent compete with an eight-year-old grandchild and be on nearly equal terms?

Play at the beach. The gentleman makes a good point and experiences the "Joy of Bocce."

Chapter 5
The Game As Played On Courts

While lawn bocce is very exciting and serves the sporting needs of a great many people, some players feel a need to advance to the next level. Playing bocce on a court with stone dust, clay or artificial surface brings the game to that higher plane. Bocce games played on courts generally take place in social clubs or in public parks. The play may be informal "pickup" games or structured as leagues. For league games between two social clubs, three games to a match is common, after which the hosts generally provide drinks and/or dinner. Increasingly, especially in areas that have no public courts, bocce lovers are building their own backyard courts (instructions in chapter 8).

As we have stated, there is a movement toward rules standardization, but so far it hasn't happened. "Official" courts are 60, 70, 80 feet and longer in different areas of the country. The court game is quite different from playing in an open park where whoever has the pallino can choose the direction to roll it. In many ways the court version of bocce is similar to the game played on lawns, but it multiplies the importance of strategy and planning moves ahead.

When my family and I play lawn bocce there's no telling where the pallino will end up. Sometimes even clever strategy goes for naught. But, on our backyard court, I know the object ball will stay somewhere within the wooden banks of the 10 x 76 foot alley. I can plan what to do with each ball accordingly. Also, playing on courts includes a new dimension of skillfully played bank shots.

Finesse is a bigger factor on courts due to the fast surface of a fine, hard packed stone dust, clay or oyster shell. The ball cruises along on a seemingly frictionless path. Since it travels such a distance with little energy supplied by the player, finesse and touch are critical. Players need to develop a smooth release of the ball and the soft touch of a basketball shooting guard to achieve success. In addition, the raffa and volo shots can be perfected on courts because the lumps, bumps and other surface abnormalities of the lawn are eliminated.

Even when played on official courts, bocce is not a physically demanding sport. Some claim physical benefits, but this is a stretch. Sure, you're using the large muscle groups of the upper and lower body, but an aerobic workout it's not. You can burn about half a calorie for each raffa shot that you take, so after a zillion games you might lose a pound. There is no pounding on your spine and knees as in basketball, no sprinting and sliding as in baseball, and no oxygen deprivation as in tennis or racquetball. You don't have to be in shape to play bocce, though physical fitness controls the fatigue factor in any competitive sport. On the other hand, the mental and social benefits of bocce are incalculable. Competing on courts or grass fosters a healthy outlook on life. And after all, bocce meets today's health and fitness standard of favoring lifetime sports over those that you can enjoy only in your youth.

Elite players maintain that fitness is a major factor in large, double elimination tournaments. Some have competed almost around the clock, from 9:00 a.m. to midnight and beyond. Furthermore, they claim that the rapid-fire shoot-out competitions held at major bocce events are among the most physically demanding endeavors in sports. Reminiscent of the NBA's three-point shoot-out, bocce's rapid-fire drill gives players the opportunity to show off their voloing ability. Competitors run from one end of the court to the other attempting to score as many hits as possible within a five-minute time limit. As you can imagine, five minutes of continuous running and tossing bocce

balls in the air can make for a very tiring exercise. {See Chapter 12 – International Play for more on the volo shoot-out.}

Initial Toss Of Pallino

The game is more structured on the court; its rules more clearly refined, if not uniform. First off, there are rules governing the initial toss of the pallino. Again, there is no standardization of the rules, it being played differently from one area to another even within the same country (see Chapter 11 for North American Open Rules, which we hope will become the standard).

Most rules specify that the pallino must travel a minimum distance – usually beyond the half-court marker and a minimum distance from the end board. Besides the required distance that the pallino must settle from the players, some rules stipulate that it come to rest a minimum distance from the side walls. The now defunct International Bocce Association, formerly of Utica, New York, developed a set of rules that are still widely used in the East. They require the first toss of pallino reach mid-court or beyond, and settle at least four feet from the endboard and 12 inches from the sideboard. If the initial toss of pallino does not satisfy all of these requirements, the pallino is returned to the player for another attempt. IBA rules give the player three attempts to successfully place the pallino, after which it goes to the other team for one attempt. If that try fails, the referee places the pallino in a legal position and play resumes. The team with pallino advantage (the one who made the

three unsuccessful attempts) still tosses the first ball. {See North American Open Rules for our recommendation on a more modern approach to the initial toss of pallino.}

Note: In recreational play, when the pallino fails to settle within legal parameters, players often agree to speed up the game by simply moving it to a legal position. For example, if the ball comes to rest eight inches from the left sideboard, they move it four inches or so to the right. If it settles three feet from the endboard, they bring it forward a foot.

Foul Lines

Official courts have foul lines that players may not step past until they release the ball. Some rules stipulate a single foul line (at each end of the court), others mandate two foul lines – one for pointing and one for hitting. The reasoning for the second foul line is that many players use a three- or four-step approach when hitting (called spocking in some areas). The pointing line does not allow enough runway for this shot, so a second hitting line, closer to the target, is used. In any case, the player must release the ball before passing the foul line. The first foot foul committed by each player results in a warning, and subsequent fouls carry penalties. Both the raffa and the volo players can use the hitting line as their release point. Standing hitters may position themselves right at the hitting line when attempting a raffa or volo.

Note: International rules mandate one line for pointing and raffa hitting, and a second for volo hitting (often, a volo approach involves even more steps than a raffa).

Pre-Game Warm-Ups

In tournaments and some recreational play, the participants roll a frame in each direction to get acclimated to the court. During this once-up and once-back practice, players attempt the various shots (punto, raffa, volo) and look for irregularities and tendencies in the surface before actual play begins. Pay close attention to how the ball rolls at various speeds. Look for any clues that might help you play various shots during the ensuing game. Play a ball or two off the sideboard to see if the carom is as you expect. Toss a raffa off the backboard to check how much bounce back you get.

Playing The Game

Regardless of the surface on which you play bocce, the roll for point is the most important skill in the game. You may be able to

survive without a raffa or volo shot, but if you cannot point, you cannot compete well in bocce. A complete player needs to be able to point *and* hit, but, just as the fastball is the king of pitches in baseball, the punto is sovereign in the kingdom of bocce.

When an opponent's point is too close to outlag, good players use the raffa or volo to try to knock it away. The ideal knockaway ball strikes its target, sends it out of contention, and then settles in for the point. Even if the hit is good but the opponent's ball is still in, at least now there should be room to close in for the score. If the shot misses its mark, however, the shooter must decide if it is worth the risk to take another knockaway shot. The percentages may be better for closing in to keep the opponent from scoring multiple points.

Some good players try to hit away a ball even though it is not extremely close. They want to have one of their team's balls at the backboard in case the opponents knock the object ball there later in the game. They reason that a good hit eliminates the opponent's point, and a miss puts a ball at the backboard acting as a kind of insurance policy. Purists say that there is too much play off the side and backboards. In some areas of the country, players look for every opportunity to take the object ball to the backboard. Then they simply pound the endboard to score points. Purists don't want the game dominated by play in the end zone; they want it played in the open court where luck is less a factor and touch is the dominating skill. "These guys think the game is billiards," commented one disgruntled bocce enthusiast unhappily watching balls carom off the back and sideboards. "Some of them even make the first toss of pallino off the side board," he added. "What game are they playing?"

Consider the following common scenario: Team A tosses pallino and brings its first ball several inches away from the target ball. Team B tries an unsuccessful raffa and elects to try a second knockaway shot. That one misses too, leaving two of Team B's balls at the end board. Team B, after some thought, attempts a third raffa, this time driving the pallino to the backboard. The raffa shot rolls to the endboard, too. Now, three of Team B's balls are in, even though only one of their shots was a hit. Scenarios such as these are spurring a movement to institute a rule stating that a ball that hits the backboard without first hitting a ball on the court is dead. The dead ball is removed from the court, and may not score a point. Again, purists want the rules to favor the player with skill and touch. Some bocce enthusiasts want to go as far as marking the position of the balls when the object ball is near the backboard or whenever a missed volo or raffa is likely. The player must then call his shot, and if he misses and displaces other balls, all balls may be returned to their original positions (bocce's *rule of advantage* would apply, in which case the opponents could elect to return the scattered balls to their original positions, or leave them in their new locations).

Most courts have a swingboard or bumpered board (see Chapter 8, Building a Backyard Court) at each end that serves to absorb the force of a ball hitting it. Again, this design is to keep players from using the backboard as a rebounding instrument, first rifling a raffa off the board, then watching it carom back toward the pallino. The idea is to entice players to score points by using the more skillful smooth roll.

Shot Selection

Before each shot, stand at the backboard and analyze the situation. Select which type of shot is appropriate for the current lay of the balls. Make a quick mental picture of the distance and layout of the previously played balls. Pause briefly to let the picture come into focus. Now form a mental image of the successful completion of the shot you will attempt. Finally, block everything else out of your mind – the score, the fans, the opponents – and execute.

The smooth roll for point is the most common shot in bocce. Most players use it and one of the two knockaway shots (raffa or volo) in their game. Currently, there are very few bocce players using the volo technique here on the East Coast. You should try to master both the raffa and volo technique. Both are a bit awkward at first, but with practice they can become successful parts of your game. When

I was first introduced to the correct rafa and volo styles, I resisted. I wasn't comfortable. "Why use a bowling-type run-up approach?" I thought. "You can't slide on a bocce court." And overstepping the foul line after releasing the ball didn't sit well with me either. But, after I built my own backyard court and practiced proper technique, the shots became natural and welcome additions to my game.

Thinking Ahead

Before choosing the type of shot to attempt, think ahead about the consequences of the shot. If I roll a ball here, what will my opponent likely do? Do I want to stay short of the target so as not to nudge the pallino toward an opponent's ball? Or do I want to be long so that I might push the pallino toward my own team's previously played ball(s). When I introduced my friend, Walter Pare, to bocce, he called the game "lawn chess". "You can think ahead and know the move you want to make" says Pare, "but you can't always place the pieces exactly where you want them."

Playing Bank Shots

One of the neat things about playing on a court is the opportunity to deftly execute bank shots. I tend to agree with the purists who want the game in the open court, away from the side and endboards. Nevertheless, a well-placed shot that caroms off the sideboard and slips in between two other balls and steals the point is one of the nicest feelings that bocce has to offer. (Note that international rules prohibit play off the side and endboards.) Bank shots are mastered by experimenting. Practice hitting the boards at different angles and at different speeds. Watch the carom and make a mental file of the results. Teach yourself this effective technique and add it to your game.

Moving The Pallino To Gain Advantage

Be aware that the position of the pallino may change at any time during a frame. A well-placed raffa or volo attempt can save the day by redirecting the pallino away from one team's balls and toward the other's. Keep this in mind during play. Consider where your opponent may try to move the pallino to gain an advantage, and how you can minimize the chance of this happening. Often, this simply means keeping a ball near the endboard to prevent the other team from scoring easy points by bringing the object ball there. Or it can mean intentionally leaving a ball short, and in front of the pallino, blocking the path of your opponents' next attempt.

Courting Bocce

Bocce may be the sleeping giant of sports. For it to really explode in America many more courts need to be constructed. The sport needs more visibility, more exposure. Promoters are looking for media coverage and corporate support for big time tournament action. They are also trying to introduce bocce into school systems, but, while permanent courts are being installed in high schools in the Midwest and West, this is being greeted with mixed results. This is reminiscent of the introduction of soccer into American schools. Officials were skeptical at first, but soccer flourishes today because people realized how inexpensive and easy it was to initiate soccer programs. The same is true for bocce.

According to demographic research done by the United States Bocce Federation, the average age of the American bocce player has decreased by almost 20 years since the 1980's (when it was age 60). The visibility of the game has increased dramatically due to the construction of outdoor facilities. Bocce is especially popular in states like California and Florida where residents play outdoors year round. Some employers are even building courts on job sites, creating a pleasant diversion for hardworking people. Installing signs that summarize the rules and give a little history of the game serves to prevent vandalism and misuse of the courts (in one California park, visitors used the bocce courts as horseshoe pits). Bocce promoters hope to get bocce courts in schools, park and recreation departments, senior centers, youth clubs, new housing developments, hospitals, and even correctional facilities. While seeking corporate and business sponsorships, the ultimate goal is to increase tournament exposure and lure the television market.

For the sport to continue its growth, it must have standardization of equipment and courts. Today bowling balls, pins, and alleys are uniform across the country. There is no reason the same consistency can't be true of bocce. See Chapter 11 – Tournament Play & Rules for recommendations.

An Alternative To Shutting Down For Winter

My "bocce posse" plays recreational bocce Monday mornings here in Eastern Massachusetts. While most bocce players tell of cookouts and wine that complement the sport, we are partial to coffee and pastry. A collection of retirees and entrepreneurial types, we play outdoors as long as we can – usually April through November. Initially, we relegated ourselves to the fact that we were going to have to switch to playing cards on Mondays until spring bocce could resume. We have no nearby indoor courts. There are lots of terrific venues in Western Massachusetts, a hot-bed of "pound the pallino to the backboard" bocce...but nothing close to home.

We worked a deal with the proprietor of a place in Lawrence, Massachusetts called Home Run Park (where baseball and softball players rent space to bat, field, and stay in shape in the off season). The facility has yards and yards of Astroturf and is not busy in the morning unless there is school vacation. A reconditioned old mill building from Lawrence's glory days, the venue is perfect for our indoor winter bocce season. Initially we just put down some two-by-fours to frame off several courts. We have evolved to setting 6" by 6" by 8' timbers end to end framing as many as four 12' by 72' courts. This might be a good option for those of you, like my group, not lucky enough to be in a warm climate or in an area populated with indoor bocce facilities.

Indoor court set-up at Home Run Park

Four courts set up at Home Run Park

Bocce Etiquette

1. Don't take too long thinking over a shot.
2. Don't over-coach or tell teammates what to do on each shot. Make suggestions. But, to execute well, a player needs to feel comfortable with the shot that he'll attempt.
3. Don't wander off – stay with the team even when you have completed delivery of your allotted bocce balls.
4. Be ready to play when it's your turn.
5. Stay under emotional control at all times.
6. Remain quiet while others take their turn.
7. After each frame, leave balls in place until the referee officially awards points.
8. Losing team buys the drinks.

Variations Of Play

In 1995 the Special Olympics World Games were held in Connecticut, and I served as one of the bocce officials. (Four years later the Games moved to North Carolina, and in 2003 to Dublin, Ireland). During the rare "down time" when we weren't officiating, we played bocce with some of the Connecticut locals. They insisted that the initial toss of the "pill" had to come to rest at least 12 inches from the side boards. If it stopped say, eight inches or so from the side, one player would give it a gentle kick into legal position (approximately 12 inches from the board) rather than roll it back to the player to try again. This kept the game moving, they reasoned. The position of the object ball (now in the same general area as the person rolling it intended) is not going to unfairly favor one team or the other.

At the North Carolina SO World Games in 1999 we encountered locals who played a fascinating variation. They favored teams of four players, each rolling one ball. Furthermore, the balls are marked 1, 2, 3, and 4. Teams must decide at the start of the game who will be first roller, second, etc. This order may not be altered during the course of play. This, they claimed, negated an outstanding player's skills. For example, a player couldn't say "Tom, you take this short. You're better at hitting than I am." The sequence can never be altered.

Another difference to their play was in the "hitting". They never rolled with speed to knock an opponent's ball away. They rolled almost as if for point, gently nudging the opponent's ball out of position and leaving their ball close to the target. Conventional wisdom is that faster speeds make for truer rolls, but it was hard to argue with the uncanny accuracy we witnessed at Fearrington Village, North Carolina.

Fearrington bocce courts, NC

Rich Mazzulla from Elmwood Park, Illinois learned to play bocce from his grandfather. "Gramps was from Italy and was an excellent player. We played to 21 points, however 3 balls closest to the object ball counted as 6 points and 4 balls closest counted as 8 points."

In this variation you get a "bonus" if you score multiple points, doubling your score for the frame. Three good rolls get you six points and four gets you eight. If you play this way, it's a good idea to play to 21.

Forty-five Degree Angle Boards?

More than a couple of "old timers" have told me about playing bocce with 45 degree angle boards at each end. You could carom your shot off these to direct your ball into scoring position. {Sounds more like billiards than bocce.}

Tom Coyle uses these 45 degree angle boards - a style of play that he picked up in Phillipsburg, New Jersey.

45° angle boards, Tucson, AZ

"I placed the corner boards, thinking all courts had them. I later found out that nobody else has them and am now considering their removal if I want better players to arrange home-and-home matches with me. But the people who play on my court absolutely love them."

To stop players from always playing off the angle and end boards, Tom made a rule that "any ball thrown to backboard without first hitting a sideboard or another ball is removed from play for that inning."

The angle boards make it "a little easier to keep the lower skilled teams in the game" and his rules discourage ricocheting balls off the back and favor pointing or "coodling in" as he calls it.

Bob Goetz of North Carolina says he's seen the 45 degree angle courts in Cleveland, Ohio. "It makes for a fun and interesting game. For example, one can ride the ball down the far right corner, and with sufficient speed, catch the left hand corner (basically reversing the direction from the start of the throw) and back to the pallino. This is a very effective shot, especially when the pallino seems surrounded heavily in the front by other balls."

Mercy/Slaughter/Skunk Rule?

Stan Stanton of Las Vegas coined the phrase "kill the skunk" when trying to eliminate a shut-out shortened game – thus preventing getting "skunked." "Colorful language for a wonderful game" he mused.

A "skunk rule" is not common in bocce but in some parts of New Hampshire, 8-0 invokes a "mercy rule" or "slaughter rule".

"If you are behind that far, you're probably overmatched, so let's get the next game going" is one perspective. And "Behind 8-0 means you are behind. It doesn't mean you've lost" is the other.

I'm the type that never gives up - a holdover from my days in the dog-eat-dog world of competitive basketball and baseball. There is nothing more exhilarating than coming back from a big deficit and winning. One baseball season, when I was coaching the local high school team, we faced a must-win situation on the final day of the season. A victory would make us conference champs, sending us to the state tourney. A loss would probably relegate us to second place. The other team jumped on us right away with multiple runs in the early innings. In short order we were down 14-1 coming to bat in the sixth inning (high school baseball hereabouts is a seven-inning affair). I got the troops together, put substitutes in the game, and said things like "Let's bat for a half-hour" and "Hey, this is gonna be a comeback story you can tell your grandchildren." Then the most incredible thing happened. We batted for 31 minutes, sending 20 batters to the plate. There were 12 hits, and 5 walks, but no errors. We ended up winning the contest and the conference championship. The non-starters that I put in when the game was seemingly out of hand went 8 for 8 - shows what a lousy coach I am. Most of the parents had gone home when we fell behind in the late innings, and our players had trouble convincing them that we had won the game.

We were part of something very special that day. Something that a "mercy rule" or "slaughter rule" would have prevented. I'm against shortening games in this manner unless you are running a large tournament and need to keep to a tight schedule.

Backboard Dead?

There is a movement afoot (a good one, I think) to make any ball that hits the backboard without first hitting another bocce ball or the pallino a "dead" ball. The ball is removed from the court and may not score a point. This is a compromise of sorts between the very strict International Rules and today's so-called Open Rules. International rules include "calling" shots, and marking the positions of previously played balls (which are returned to their original positions if the caller fails to make an accurate shot). Even top players think that the international rules are a "tough sell" for most recreational players in this country. Critics claim that international play is too complicated and makes the game long and dull.

The movement though, is toward making the game one of touch and finesse, while minimizing the luck factor. In the East where many play everything "live" off the backboard, early in a frame they often attempt to hit away an opponent's close point. If they miss, they reason, "That's okay. I wanted a ball at the back anyway, in case the opposition knocks the pallino there later." With the backboard always live, a poor shot can come into play later.

In some areas they play the back wall dead no matter how a ball got there. Say you try to knock away a close point and miss. If your missed attempt hits the backboard, it is dead (taken out of the court and not figured in the scoring for that frame). If your shot successfully hits its target and causes the struck ball to hit the back wall, then that ball is dead. Furthermore, if you hit your target causing it to roll to the back and your ball has sufficient momentum so that it too hits the back, then it also is dead.

I think that somewhere in bocce's past (all of these games - bocce, bowls, boules - have their evolution lost in the mists of antiquity) the game was played with ditches at both ends. Causing an opponent's ball to end up in the ditch was a big advantage - it couldn't score a point.

Part of me likes this idea that you play the home team's rules when you visit their court, and they play your rules when they come to your venue. It's part of the charm and fascination of the game. The variations are testimony to the enduring appeal of an activity that evolved in different parts of the world, is played somewhat differently from place to place, yet whose basic idea is the same. Let's see who can roll, toss or otherwise deliver their bocce balls closest to the object ball.

Yet, another part of me cries out for standardization so that the game can advance to the level of say, professional bowling. Hey, I like bowling, but bocce has it all over bowling. It has a cerebral aspect that I don't see in just knocking pins down. If bowling can achieve such a high level, there is no reason bocce can't as well.

Chapter 6
The Equipment ▰▰▰▰▰▰▰▰▰▰▰▰▰▰▰▰

One of the neat things about bocce is that you need very little equipment to enjoy the game. All you require is a set of bocce balls that, with proper care, can last a lifetime. Be aware, though, that top players purchase new sets several times a year. Reasoning that a couple nicks and scratches on a ball's surface could alter its path to the target, they aren't taking any chances. And, at the other end of the competitive spectrum, many recreational, backyard lawn players use an "anything goes" style of play where the object ball is "live" no matter where it ends up (in the woods, ravine, creek, stream, just about anywhere). As you might expect, more than a few pallinos get lost and need to be replaced.

Sure, there are designer shoes and apparel and exotic measuring devices, but these are extras. My family and friends played backyard bocce for years with nothing more than a good set of bocce balls. We didn't even own a fancy measuring device. The points that we couldn't call by eye we measured with our feet, hands, twigs, string, an old car antenna or a standard tape measure. For many of us, though, bocce becomes almost an obsession. We want to read and learn more about it, practice and play more often, and explore bocce related paraphernalia. What follows is a brief primer on the equipment, the publications, and their distributors. There are some pretty neat gadgets and bocce gear that make terrific gifts for the bocce buff in your life. I've spent a good deal of time and effort evaluating equipment, and have become a distributor for those items I am comfortable endorsing. You can purchase or learn more about these at www.joyofbocce.com. Most of the products distributed via my site I "drop ship" rather than inventory. In almost every instance the price to the consumer will be the same whether you purchase the item from the manufacturer/dealer or from me. So, you could purchase directly from them and they'd keep ALL of the money. Or, you could purchase from my site at the same price and they'd only keep MOST of the money, (and you'd be supporting our efforts at *The Joy of Bocce*).

Bocce Balls

First off, don't buy an inferior set just to save a few dollars. The balls may be the only bocce-related purchase you'll ever make, so it should be a cost-effective one. A good quality set will cost you in the neighborhood of $100 or more and may include a warranty of up to five years. Bocce balls are commonly 4 ¼ inches in diameter and weigh about two pounds, with specifications varying slightly from one manufacturer to another (metric equivalents are 100 to 120 mm and 900 to 1100 grams). The pallino is approximately 2 1/8 inches (55-60 mm) in diameter, but some sets come with a smaller 1 ½ inch (36-41 mm) object ball. Most dealers package a set of eight balls and a pallino. This usually includes four balls of one color, four of another color, and a pallino of a third color. Bocce balls traditionally were made of wood, but today are of composition material much like bowling balls (some international play mandates metal balls). Some sets further distinguish the four balls of each color with engraved marks to tell one teammate's balls from another. This is of dubious advantage since telling which teammate threw which ball is not nearly as important as telling which team's ball is which.

If you are going to play exclusively on grass, try to avoid the smaller object balls. Small pallinos tend to be obscured even by closely cropped lawns. My family has used a croquet ball or field hockey ball as the object ball when playing on grass, and the bocce pallino when we're on the court. Some manufacturers include a carrying case with the set of balls, others make it an extra. Careful – some of the more expensive European balls come four to a set instead of eight and don't include a pallino (and metal balls are sold in sets of two). Really competitive players cart their personal bocce balls wherever they play. They want the consistency that using the same bocce balls every game brings. You'll see them use a cloth or chamois to wipe dust and debris from the ball before each toss.

Bocce Ball Dealers

Many U.S. sporting goods manufacturers and dealers offer bocce sets for sale. You will find bocce balls under the names of outfits like SportCraft, Eddie Bauer, Classic Sports, and Regent Sports. You can visit the sporting goods departments at places like Bradlee's, K-Mart, and Wall-Mart, but be advised that the popularity of bocce in your area will have an impact on the store's inventory. We conducted a telephone survey in northeastern Massachusetts to determine which department stores stocked bocce equipment. More than a few of those answering the phones had never heard of bocce, and connected us with the lawn and garden/camping department to talk about "hibachis." Department store bocce sets may have been made in, and imported from China or Taiwan.

Italian Bocce Balls

CAST, Salf, Super Martel and Perfetta are well regarded Italian-made bocce balls. Salf and Super Martel are not readily available in this country as of this printing, but CAST and Perfetta balls are available via several web sites including www.joyofbocce.com.

Perfetta bocce balls have a great reputation for quality and exacting measurement standards. Perfetta offers sets for true international competition as well as those for recreational play. High end "Professional" sets are sold in sets of four (you bring your set and your opponent brings his/hers).

*Perfetta bocce set in traditional red
and green w/carry bag*

International punto, raffa, volo rules state that bocce balls must be 107 mm in diameter with a weight of 920 grams. The pallino must be 40 mm in diameter and weigh 60 grams. (Women and juniors under 14 may use balls of 106 mm in diameter weighing 900 grams). Though you may never play international rules, the 107 mm size should be your first criterion in selecting bocce balls. Unless you have large hands, balls bigger than 107 mm tend to be too large to control easily, especially with volo shooting. Some balls are as large as 115 mm or more.

If you want to save a few bucks, look for American manufacturers who make bocce balls to the same specs as the Perfetta balls. One such outfit is Epco, located in Medway, Massachusetts. Many bowling ball manufacturers are "retooling" for bocce, recognizing the growth of the sport, and hoping to "get a piece of the action".

A Word About Playing Rules That Accompany Your Purchase

There are different sets of rules that govern bocce play in America. The only rules that are standardized are the true international rules discussed in chapter 12. Any set of rules that comes with your purchase should be taken for what it is – a set of rules. Various groups, trying to gain a foothold in the sport, have made deals with manufacturers to insert their version of the rules and court dimensions into each bocce set sold. One mandates a 60-by 12-foot court (short by many other groups' standards). The point is that these are one group's "official" specifications for the game. There are others. Consider our chapters 8 and 11 before accepting any group's court layout or playing rules as law.

Bocce Carry Bag

If, for some reason, you have a set of bocce balls but need a carry bag, I recommend one of heavy duty nylon material. These are generally 9" X 9" X 9", and hold 8 balls and 1 pallino. Most feature a zipper and perhaps a velcro closure - view current pricing at www. joyofbocce.com. Some dealers offer metal, plastic or wooden crates, but the nylon bag is the way to go.

Bocce Ball Polish

Maybe you'll want to shine 'em up instead of buy a new set. This product is specially formulated for cleaning and polishing bocce or bowling balls. It restores shine and superior grip for high performance, and the non-abrasive formula will not harm ball surface. See www.joyofbocce.com for current pricing.

Measuring Devices

In informal recreational bocce, you can get by without a formal measuring device, using hands, feet, string, twigs, car antenna, or other household objects to determine points. Most families have a standard tape measure in the garage or workshop, and that works very well, especially for long measurements. We recommend metric measurements over English. When comparing very similar lengths, gauging centimeters is easier than calculating eighths and sixteenths of an inch. Be advised though, that some bocce measures have no calibrations. We don't need to know the actual distance between the balls in contention and the pallino, just which one is shorter. The ever-ready tape measure is a staple at most spirited bocce games. Often, the sport produces something akin to a football huddle – a crowd engulfing the object ball anxiously awaiting the results of a measurement.

Measuring Via Geometry

Believe it or not, you can skip the measuring device and use the Pythagorean Theorem to determine which ball is in. Stand by the bocce balls and form a triangle with the object ball (pallino) at the apex (see photo).

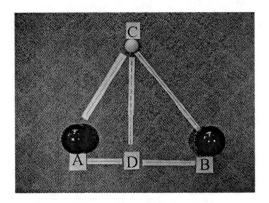

1) Draw an imaginary line (A - B) between the two bocce balls (see photo - RED to the left, GREEN to the right).

2) Now draw an imaginary perpendicular (C - D) from the pallino to line segment AB

3) Since AD is obviously shorter than DB, then AC has to be shorter than BC...so the RED ball is in. If you had known this strategy in high school, I bet you would have tried to stay awake in geometry class. This might also indicate, as previously suspected, that the ancient Greeks played some serious bocce.

People send me many photos of bocce players measuring for points with various tape measures. Usually they are holding one end of the tape at the pallino, then extending the tape over the top center of the ball being measured (or vice-versa). This is okay to get a general idea of which ball is closer, but for accuracy you need *inside measure*. Place the tape measure between the object ball and bocce ball and see how much tape needs to be extended between the two.

There are many measuring devices specifically designed for the ball-and-target games of bocce, boules, and lawn bowls. Following are some that we've tested and recommend.

Remember: when measuring for point in bocce, we don't have to know the actual distance in inches or centimeters. We just need to know which ball is closer to the object ball.

Premier Boule Measure

This is a small, slender metric tape measure that extends to two meters (more than six feet). The tape is self-locking when extended, and to retract it you have to press a release button on top. It is best to hold on to the tape as you press the button to ensure that the internal rewind mechanism does not get fouled. There are no calibrations on the steel tape. We aren't measuring the actual distance between the balls, just determining which one is closer.

A thin plastic post extends about a centimeter from the back end of the measure. When measuring, this post is placed against the pallino. To use this device, place it on the ground between the pallino and the ball in question. Place the rear post against the pallino and extend the tape until it touches the bocce ball. The tape will remain extended to this length. Move over to the other bocce ball in contention, and compare.

This measure has calipers for evaluating shorter lengths. The calipers extend from the base of the measure and fold neatly out of the way when not in use. And if all of this is not enough for you, the implement will even keep score. On one side, it has a clever spinning wheel arrangement that tracks two team's scores up to 21. Available at *www.joyofbocce. com*.

The Premier Boule Measure

Clubhawk Gold Bowls Measure

Using a string rather than a steel tape, this is an extremely accurate measuring device (popular with lawn bowls players in England). It extends a couple feet farther than the Premier, has the same calipers for close measurements, and even has a belt clip.

Remember, we don't need a finely calibrated instrument that measures exactly how far a ball is from the object ball...we just need to know which is closer to it. This nifty string device does the trick. You pull out enough string to reach the first ball you are measuring. If you have to pull more string from the housing to reach the other ball in contention... then it is farther away! Available at *www. joyofbocce.com*.

The Clubhawk Gold Bowls Measure

Henselite Bowls Measure

This is a small metal telescopic device not much bigger than a ball point pen (approximately six inches when closed). The ingenious tool is for inside measurement. The player or referee first estimates the distance between the pallino and the two bocce balls to be compared. Then, he extends the appropriate

The Henselite Bowls Measure

telescopic sections to a length slightly less than that estimate. Next, he places the device between the pallino and one of the balls in question and extends it until it touches both balls. The head of the tool is equipped with a screw-top mechanism. Turning the top in one direction lengthens the tool, while winding in the opposite direction shortens it. This fine-tuning makes for very precise measuring. Finally, the measurer places the device between the pallino and the other ball and compares. Extra care must be taken with this device.

The Henselite Bowls Measure in use

A careless person might easily disturb the positions of balls being measured.

Like a ball point pen, the Henselite Bowls Measure has a clasp for fastening onto your shirt pocket. Fully extended, it is one meter (approximately 39 inches) long, so you'll still need a tape for longer measures. For measurements less than the length of the tool, it has calipers that fold out of the way when not needed. These calipers are capable of measuring 1/8 inch to 6 inches. Available at <u>www.joyofbocce.com</u>.

Standard Carpenter's Rule

Another excellent and easy-to-obtain measuring device is the standard carpenter's rule. Available at any hardware store in 6' and 8' lengths, look for the rule that includes the 6" sliding metallic extension. This sliding extension makes the tool ideal for bocce measurements. Unfold the rule to a length that fits between the two balls. Now place the rule on the ground with the back end touching the pallino, and slide the extension forward until it touches the ball being measured. Carefully lift the rule, and reposition it to compare the other ball in contention.

*Carpenter's rule - note sliding
extension*

The Resolver

Finally, a measure that deserves mention is *The Resolver*, cleverly designed by Mike Paccione of Cresskill, New Jersey. The Resolver is a tape measure set atop a clear acrylic cube that fits over the pallino. The tape (metric and English units) swivels 360 degrees and extends over two meters. The instructions that come with the device tell you to "extend the tape to one of the larger balls in dispute

The Resolver

and lock it by pressing the bottom of the red power lock. Swivel the extended tape to the other ball(s) in dispute. If the tape does not reach the other ball(s), then the first ball is nearest the pallino. If it touches any other ball, then it is nearest. (Use of the measuring scale on top is optional.)" Direct inquiries to *The Resolver*, P.O. Box 535, Cresskill, NJ 07626 or mike2222@optonline.net.

Some of the top players frown on the device, claiming that it is not accurate enough for high level play. They reason that it is too difficult to center the cube over the pallino and this leads to inaccuracy. The truest measurement is "inside measure" using a device like the Premier Boule, Clubhawk Gold, or Henselite Bowls Measure described above. The reasoning may be true, but for most casual play this ingenious device is more than adequate. It is quick and easy and even makes it unlikely that you'll inadvertently disturb the positions of balls while measuring. Many bocce players determine points using a tin can and string (can fits over the pallino and string extends from center of overturned can). The Resolver is far superior to that.

While all of the measures described above are excellent, you may still want a conventional tape measure for determining points that are farther than a couple meters from the pallino. And take heart, soon I'm sure there will be a low frequency laser activated bocce measure.

Scoreboards

Peter Rabito (President of Bulldog Bocce Products) of the Long Island Bocce Club has designed customized metallic scoreboards that are 12" by 18" by 48" that stick into the ground and can be removed and put away after playing. Each clock face scorer is mounted on a ground stake, is transportable, weighs less than 10 lb., and comes fully assembled. For more information or to order, email Peter directly at Bulldogbocce@optonline.net or prabito@rainbow-media.com or call him at 631-807-4030.

*Example of
Bulldog Bocce
Scoreboard*

Tom McNutt of Boccemon.com pitches four scoreboard ideas via his excellent web site.

1) He features a bocce scoreboard t-shirt that uses Velcro buttons – you can keep score right on your shirt. According to Boccemon "No longer do you have to rely on fatigued brain cells to remember the score. Point to your mobile scoreboard."

2) He also offers an inexpensive personal clip-on scorekeeper. According to McNutt "...at one time bocce was condemned by the Catholic Church and clergymen were forbidden to play the game. Imagine the Priests at the Abbey keeping score with their rosary or "sacrifice" beads...Here's how it works... simply slide a bead down for each point. When the game is over, slide the beads back to the top and start a new game."

3) The Skorstik works like a vertical cribbage board. (If the score is "6" there will be a cork in the sixth hole for the appropriate team). Use it for most any field sport, including Bocce, Soccer, Lacrosse, or Field Hockey.

4) Boccemon also offers a scoreboard "built with serious Bocce players in mind". The aluminum signboard mounts easily to a 2" pipe, providing "Excellent visibility for players and spectators. Ideal for all weather conditions." See www.boccemon.com for more photos and current prices or email him at Tom@boccemon.com.

Rico Daniele of WWOBA (Wonderful World of Bocce Association, 800-BOCCE54) offers two styles of scoreboards, one 3' by 4' made of heavy duty plastic and another metallic one that measures 4' by 8'. View his web site at *www.playbocce.com* for more info and current pricing.

103

WWOBA scoreboard in background

David Brewer at BocceBrew.com offers two scoreboards that measure 3' long by 10" tall. One is heavy gauge aluminum with 3M vinyl paint and the other is kiln dried redwood with polyurethane coating and 3M vinyl paint. Magnetic balls travel on a steel rod to keep score. Contact Brewer at http://www.boccebrew.com (415-461-8842).

Court Maintenance Tools

I've seen all kinds of home-made court maintenance brushes and scrapers. Two things have always struck me about them. 1 – they look like they are home-made, and 2 – they tend to be HEAVY.

Drag Brush

Lee Tennis, (makers of the Har-Tru court surface material) is now marketing their tennis court maintenance tools to bocce players. Although originally created for tennis, they are ideal for bocce. I love their 7-foot drag brush. It is light-weight and, even if you have a 13- or 14-foot wide court, you can smooth it over with just two passes. This is quick enough to do between games without forcing anxious players to stand around waiting. Bristles are 4 ½ inches of synthetic fibers and the strong but light-weight frame is aluminum. Available via www.joyofbocce.com.

7' Drag Brush

Lute/Scarifier

This handy, light-weight metal rake-like tool is excellent for grooming bocce courts. The 30" wide device is actually two tools in one. It is an all-aluminum combination tool for scarifying, leveling, and removing loose court material. Strong and sturdy, the tool is light enough to handle with ease and is excellent for spreading new material during top-dressing. The concave shape of the 30" wide blade allows the tool to "float" along the surface without digging in. Use the serrated edge to scrape material from high spots, then flip the tool over to rake and smooth that spot and drag the loose material to fill in a lower point. Available via www.joyofbocce.com.

Lute/Scarifier

Portable Bocce Courts

Chris Pfeiffer of Backyard Bocce has developed a clever line of portable bocce courts. If you like playing on the lawn in a kind of "anything goes" style (I like this too!), you don't need a portable court. But, if you want a little more structure, or maybe want to run a backyard tournament, these ingenious courts are the answer. The three courts described below are 12' by 60" and can be set up on grass or dirt.

Vinyl Boundary Courts (Templates)

Set-up is not unlike pitching a tent. You stretch out the template, pull it tight with bungee cords, then drive a couple of stakes into the ground. Next, plant some flags indicating end lines and half court (visual landmarks), and you are set to go within five minutes. Foul lines are demarcated by green and red vinyl sewn into the material ten feet from each end.

There is an inexpensive, one-inch vinyl boundary court which works well, but for another twenty bucks the two-incher is a better deal – presenting a much clearer visual for players and spectators.

*One-inch vinyl
boundary court*　　　*Two-inch vinyl
boundary court*

Although many of us like longer courts, most Special Olympics bocce (for which the product was originally created) is on 12' by 60' of real estate. The decision to opt for these dimensions is probably a good one for backyard play. I also like the fact that there is just one foul line at each end (10' from the end) rather than one line for hitting and another for pointing. Also, midcourt (30') is clearly marked to indicate minimum distance the pallino must travel to begin each frame.

These two products are more boundaries than they are courts. They simply demarcate a 12' by 60' rectangle for play. Any ball that rolls or is knocked out of the rectangle is out of play – a "dead ball."

Two-inch court in use at senior center

Vinyl Mesh Court

Now if you always wanted a court with sideboards but didn't want to spend a thousand bucks or more... or you don't want to give up a permanent part of your real estate, the vinyl mesh court is your solution. It features 6" mesh sideboards and can be taken down after play, and it stores in a large carry bag.

Vinyl mesh court materials

Set-up is a little more involved, but not daunting. The written directions are clear and well illustrated, and you need only a cordless drill and a mallet. With all these products, I recommend dropping the wheels on your lawnmower, and cutting the grass before play (at least over the section where you'll place the court). Sometimes "standard" size pallinos get obscured by the grass. You may want to use a larger target. A croquet or field hockey ball works nicely. In a pinch, use a baseball or any ball about the size of a baseball.

For a more complete description of these courts see chapter 8 which has a section devoted to portable courts. Portable Courts available via *www.joyofbocce.com* - check there for current pricing.

Portable court with mesh sideboards set up on level surface

Publications

There are five internationally acclaimed bocce publications: *United States Bocce, Bocce Bowls* (Australia), *Sport-Boule* (France), *Sportbocce* (Italy), and *La Suisse Bouliste* (Switzerland). The quarterly *United States Bocce* (a United States Bocce Federation publication) includes information on the bocce scene, playing tips, tournament dates, and other valuable information. Recognized by the United States Amateur Athletic Union (A.A.U.), the Federation International de Boules, and the Confederazione Boccistica Internationale, the USBF communicates with boules, pétanque, and lawn bowling groups worldwide.

Videos

Bruce A. Moody of American Production Services, LLC (Fort Mill, SC) has produced *Let's Play Bocce!* (running time 45 minutes).

Billed as "the essential beginner's videoguide," *Let's Play Bocce!* is just that. It includes sections on the history of bocce, the court and equipment, playing the game, ball deliveries and more. It brings together the information a newcomer to the sport needs to get started. This professionally produced tape fills a niche, introducing beginners to the great game of bocce. Available at www.joyofbocce.com.

Bocce My Way, a production of Phil Ferrari's World Bocce League, is a 20-minute video which is part promotional, part instructional. It features former Miss Teen USA Laura Siler demonstrating play along with Ferrari. Together, they explain the game while demonstrating shots and proper technique. To order, visit www.worldbocce.org or contact Ferrari at 1-800-OKBOCCE (email: mrbocce@worldbocce.org).

Other Paraphernalia & Novelty Items

One of the big promoters of bocce on the East Coast, Rico Daniele of WWOBA sells bocce balls, measuring devices, other bocce related items and a line of sportswear bearing his striking bocce logo. WWOBA's product catalog includes bocce scoreboards, mugs, travel bags, and a mini bocce table game played with marbles. Daniele's book, titled *Bocce, A Sport For Everyone*, includes everything from lists of upcoming bocce stars to recipes like pallino meatballs and fettucine a la bocce. In an effort to involve school children, Daniele has created a set of bocce cartoon character prints that relate to the planets of our solar system. One bocce character is portrayed in a 24-foot parade balloon.

WWOBA bocce character parade balloon

Daniele has even brokered a deal with a Keene, NH bottler to create soft drinks, tea, and water with his bocce character logos on the label. His private label, 12-oz. "Bocce Planetary Drinks" include Bocce Ball Orange, Bocce Brew  Root Beer, Bocce Vanilla Cream Soda, Bocce Brew Sarsaparilla, Bocce Brewed Lemon Iced Tea, Bocce Natural Sparkling Water,

Bocce Bottled Spring Water and other flavors. Call Rico at 1-800-BOCCE54 for details or to order. Or email him at BOCCE54@aol.com.

Bocce Ball Retriever

Gene Youtsey and Don Allen are big time bocce fans from Myrtle Beach, South Carolina. They play on the beach at low tide, tossing the pallino out in any direction and getting their daily exercise walking the course through tidal pools and sand bars. Gene, partial to bocce over all other sports says it "beats the hell out of golf - don't cost nothin." With a wink, he's quick to add "Our groundskeeper comes in twice a day." His partner Don wants outsiders to understand that their beach bocce is not without conflict. "We play under duress that helps us when we travel to tournaments." The problem, he maintains, is that beach play requires great powers of concentration, because "...there are good looking women in bikinis everywhere."

Gene has a nagging backache making it difficult for him to bend over and pick up objects. Together with Don he developed a unique "bocce ball retriever." The device has what looks like a Tupperware bowl attached to a telescoping rod that can be adjusted to the user's height. With a little practice you can get a deft little wrist snap going, and pick up your bocce ball without bending or stooping. The South Carolina duo retails the device. Email Gene at gyoutsey@sc.rr.com.

Bocce ball retrievers
(telescopic)

Promotional Items

If you are looking for bocce t-shirts, caps, mugs, etc. you need to check out CafePress.com.

Probably the best-kept fundraising secret in the country, CafePress is smart, simple to manage, and appropriate for anybody who might want to sell promotional items for their business, hobby, club, or sports team. It's a print-on-demand company which has allowed many of us to set up "virtual storefronts". You can go to CafePress.com and search "bocce" to find stores featuring items from travel mugs to mouse pads to clothing. Or you can go directly to CafePress.com/joyofbocce to find items with the striking Joy of Bocce logo. CafePress handles all the inventory, printing, shipping and funds transfer. (To learn more about how CafePress works, see Chapter 10, Organizing A League/Promoting the Game).

Bocce Web Sites

When I first started on the World Wide Web in 1997, a search for "bocce" produced little or no results. Today, the query will return page after page of related sites. Too numerous to mention all, here are a couple of important ones (in no particular order).

www.bocce.com - United States Bocce Federation

The United States Bocce Federation is the only U.S. group recognized by the Amateur Athletic Union (A.A.U.) as well as the international bocce associations. Their web site has excellent sections

on the "Skills of Bocce" including tips on pointing and hitting technique. The site also lists tournament dates and information on qualifiers for United States Bocce Federation members who want to represent our country in World Championships. Email: bocce@juno. com.

www.Ibocce.com - **Bryan Mero**

Bryan Mero is an enthusiastic West Coast promoter of bocce. His web site is well-crafted and complete – includes info on bocce products,
courts, rules, and upcoming events. His Bocce Locations page lets you click on the postal code for a state (e.g. AZ for Arizona, WI for Wisconsin) to find courts. Also posted are 8-, 16-, and 32-team double elimination tourney brackets. Mero even offers an excellent, illustrated guidebook on building a low budget bocce court. Email Mero at: bmero@ix.netcom.com.

www.playbocce.com - www.sites2c.com/bocce/

Wonderful World of Bocce Association (WWOBA)

President Rico Daniele (899 Main Street, Springfield, MA 01103 - Phone: 1-800-BOCCE54) offers two web sites featuring a
large line of bocce-related products, instructions on building your own court, architectural blueprints for court construction, and apparel with his intricate bocce logo.

www.worldbocce.org - **World Bocce Association**

President Phil Ferrari (188 Industrial Drive 17A, Elmhurst, IL 60126 - Phone: 630-834-8349, 1-800-OKBOCCE). Web site promotes products including Ferrari's video (*Bocce My Way)*, and his World Bocce League. Email: mrbocce@worldbocce.org.

www.boccemon.com - **Tom McNutt**

Tom McNutt is a bocce court builder in the Pacific Northwest. He offers some excellent bocce products on his web site as  well as sound information on court construction. His "Bocce Tour 02" chronicles his family's two-week vacation/quest for bocce courts on the west coast and is one of the "must see" bocce attractions on the web.

Email: Tom@boccemon.com.

Other Outdoor Games

Since bocce aficionados often have an affinity for outdoor games, I've assembled some items of interest. I've located a gem of a series of Outdoor Games books by talented author Steven Boga. He's written short, well crafted, clearly illustrated books on Horseshoes, Croquet, Badminton, Volleyball, and Archery.

For those who would sooner watch the video than read the book, *Let's Play Bocce! Let's Play Horseshoes! Let's Play Croquet!* and *Let's Play Badminton!* are available. You can find all of these Outdoor Games items at www.joyofbocce.com.

Various types of bocce balls used in the last 150 years
(photo courtesy of United States Bocce Federation)

Chapter 7
Strategy & Tactics ▬▬▬▬▬▬▬▬▬▬▬

Someone once described bocce as "a game where you throw large balls toward a smaller target ball." That's like saying a fine aged wine is just some old grapes. Bocce involves skill, finesse, strategy, a plan of attack, and the ability to adjust that plan during play. The nuances of play raise it above those games that require only physical skills to be successful.

Some of the strategy discussed in this chapter is better suited for play on enclosed courts, and other applies more to open area play. The more experience you have playing on different courts and surfaces, the better instincts you will develop for employing the appropriate tactics. Become a student of the game by observing the play of teammates and opponents, especially cagey veterans. If you get "burned" by a particular strategy, file the data in your memory for future reference. Perhaps you can use it to "toast" an opponent sometime down the line. Above all, don't allow yourself to be defeated by the same tactics in the future.

Pre-Game Strategy

In most tournament play, the participants play two mock frames (one in each direction) before each game begins. This allows players to get a feel for the surface, and to gauge how the ball is likely to break in one direction or another. Phil Ferrari, of the World Bocce Association, suggests testing the rolling pattern of a court in the following manner. Divide the length of the court in thirds – an imaginary line four feet from each sideboard will create three narrow lanes on a 12-foot wide court. For wider or narrower courts, move your imaginary lines accordingly. Roll as many balls as you are allowed pre-game on all the courts on which you will compete, and watch the glide path. Roll some balls with sufficient speed to make them reach or approach the endboard, and make note of any break in their glide path. Remember that a slow moving ball will be more susceptible to this break than a fast moving one. Roll some at different speeds in each of the lanes and note the results. Test out a few bank shots and observe the angle at which the ball comes off the board. Try a few raffa (fast moving) and volo (aerial) shots, if they are in your repertoire (and permitted in the event). Get a feel for the alley and determine what form you are in. Make adjustments.

A longtime coach, I am amazed by the number of intelligent athletes who fail to monitor their game-time performance and make adjustments. As a youth, I played basketball with an exceptional scholar-athlete who possessed a feathery-soft shooting touch. Though he was multi-talented and very bright (combined 1400+ SAT scores), he sometimes failed to make critical adjustments. During one game in which he bounced his first half-dozen shots off the front rim, our coach (who probably scored 1000 points less on his SATs), called time out and made a suggestion. "When your shots fall short," he offered, "shoot harder. Try sighting on the back rim." The hooper knocked down most of the rest of his shots, and we went on to win the ball game.

Do all of this practice and adjustment-making on all of your lanes and repeat the procedure from the opposite end of the court. You may want to record your findings in a small notebook. For future reference, you may want to keep a log of all the places you play, but be aware that grooming changes will affect play. Use this pre-game technique every time you play on a court to see if the ball reacts as it did the last time you played there. Some people speak of a court having its own personality and, while home court advantage is a controversial notion in some sports, it's for real in bocce. In social club league games the more talented team generally wins, but the short odds are often on the host team.

The Lineup Card

A good player needs to be skilled in all phases of the game. Every player on the team should be able to point and hit. A player can't be a specialist, competent in only one area. Nevertheless, what follows is our suggestion for filling out your team's lineup card.

In a four-person team, the leadoff player is usually selected for his pointing ability. He or she is the one with the best touch. Some refer to a good pointer as a six-incher, implying that no matter where the pallino, s/he will roll a ball six inches or closer to it. For most of us this is simply wishful thinking. A player able to regularly roll a ball even 12 to 18 inches from the pallino is very skilled.

The number two player is generally chosen for raffa or volo ability. This player can knock away an opponent's point that is too difficult to outlag (or strike the pallino, sending it to a position more advantageous to his team). The fast rolling ball (raffa) or aerial delivery (volo) is this player's forte.

The number three player is selected for versatility. This player may be called upon to point, or knock away an opponent's ball or the pallino.

Finally, the number four player is the captain. He or she is generally skilled in all shots, has leadership qualities and the people skills not only to set strategy with teammates, but to act as spokesperson in dealings with tournament officials and referees.

Shot Selection

The key in higher levels of bocce competition is not only mastering the techniques of punto, raffa and volo, but knowing when to use each. When the opponents' shot settles in for a good point, sometimes it is better to try to outlag it, while at other times a knockaway shot is in order. Of course, we have to clarify what we mean by a good point. One foot away (or less) from the pallino is a good point. So is two feet away. A ball two feet in front of the pallino can be a very good point – much better than a ball two feet to the side. A shot even three or four feet away that is in front is always a good point. The other thing to consider when deciding on hitting or pointing is the skill of the player. How good is he at hitting vs. pointing? Think ahead in all situations, asking yourself "What is likely to happen if my shot is successful?" and "What might happen if I miss?" A big factor in the choice of shots is how many balls the other team still has to play. And always bear in mind that any ball, your own or your opponent's, may change the pallino's position. Theoretically, an eight point swing could occur. Four points for their team could become four for your team with one skillful (or lucky) redirection of the object ball.

Court Surface

The court surface can come into play when deciding strategy and what type of shot to attempt. The kind of surface and its state of grooming need to be considered. Recently groomed courts tend to be faster than those that have been played on for a while. How hard or soft the surface is will affect a volo shot that lands short of its target. Rather than hit and then roll into its target, your volo on a hard packed surface may bounce right over it. This may lead you to select the raffa over the aerial knockaway shot.

Placing The Pallino

One of the crucial strategies in bocce is intelligent placement of the pallino. Having "pallino advantage" gives you the opportunity to go to your team's strengths or to attack your opponents' weaknesses. Of course, a big key is knowing your strong points and their weaknesses. After a few frames, a clever tactical player knows his opponents' weak spots and tries to deliver the pallino there. Rather than pitch or toss the pallino out on the fly, roll it smoothly as if you were pointing. Watch its glide path. Read its motion left or right. Use this information on your following roll(s).

Many players start a frame by tossing the pallino rather willy-nilly, with an overhand, underhand, even between the legs or behind the back delivery. This is fine if you just want to get the round started, and don't care where the target ball ends up or how it got there. But, at a more competitive level, things get a little more cerebral. Remember, having pallino advantage allows you to play to your team's strength or to the opponents' weakness. Similarly, you might be able to avoid the opponents' strong suit. For example, if the other team plays exceptionally well on long rolls, try to place the object ball the minimum distance down court.

Again, roll the object ball in the same manner that you will roll your first bocce ball and from the same spot. Moreover, carefully track the pallino's path, making note of any movement before it comes to rest. When you roll the pallino hold a bocce ball in your other hand so that you can keep the same foot placement and roll that ball exactly as you did the jack.

Note: Some players, when trying to outlag an opponent's ball, like to have a ball in each hand. This is for balance, and so that feet placement can be maintained if the first attempt is unsuccessful. Instead of missing a shot, turning around to collect another ball for the next roll, then re-establishing a starting position, etc., you are already set to go. This is not allowed in international play. All balls must be in the ball rack except for the one in the hand of the person who is about to roll. This makes it easier for players and referees to see how many balls are still to be played (just check the rack).

If the target ball "fell" to the right as it rolled down the court, you can start your bocce ball out a little more left to compensate. {Note: some recommend that when a court's surface has variations that influence the roll of a ball, players should move their starting point in the direction that the ball falls.}

Let the pallino come to rest, then try to establish the initial point by rolling your first ball as close as possible to that target – in front (a tad short) is always better than long and/or left or right. When the point is in front of the object ball it provides "nuisance value" as opponents have to negotiate around it and may inadvertently tap is closer to the pallino.

If you are partial to bank shots, you may want to aim the pallino close to a sideboard. But be aware that a point that is close to pallino, but up against the sideboard, is a relatively easy target. A smart player will make a nice transfer of energy shot, hitting your ball away and leaving his in its place. If your opponents are expert at bank shots, you may want to place the object ball in the open court where they will not attempt rebound shots. The problem with spending time perfecting bank shots is that when you travel to other courts, the boards don't always respond predictably. Also, if you aspire to international style play, bank shots are not allowed.

The First Roll – Initial Point

While it is customary for the person who tossed the pallino to roll the first ball, in high levels of play it is often the captain who places the object ball. He then stands aside as his point man sets the initial point. According to highly regarded US player Dr. Angel Cordano, "At international level the pallino can be tossed by anyone and usually it is the best player who does it, to assure the position that's most advantageous for the team."

While accurate hitting is extremely important, and versatility a necessity, rolling for point is the critical skill in bocce. After all, the game evolved from the basic contest of two people trying to outdo each other tossing balls toward a target. If there were a big league bocce draft, great pointers would go in the first round. A player whose shots consistently cozy up to the pallino is in very high demand.

On the first roll establishing the initial point, you have been very successful if it takes your opponent two balls to beat it. If it takes the opposition three or four balls to outlag or knock your ball out of contention, you have been extremely successful, and your team should win the frame. The more balls your opponent uses in his attempt to outdo your initial roll, the better your chance of taking the last shot of the frame. Many players consider the first and second rolls the most critical ones since they will have an impact on who will play the last ball. When you get the last shot (the *hammer*, as shuffleboard players call it), you have an opportunity to win the frame. Big time college basketball coaches preach the philosophy of working hard to stay in the game so that in the final seconds, their team has a chance to win. That's the goal – to have the opportunity to win the game, even if it is with the last possession. Forcing your opponent to use several balls to beat your initial roll increases your chance of having the hammer. Possessing the hammer gives you the opportunity to win.

Most players like to leave the initial point a tad short rather than long. This presents problems for the opponent, as he must navigate around it, and might even inadvertently bump it closer to the target.

Leaving your initial point in front is also good news for your hitter in case your point gets outlagged by the opponents. Your hitter doesn't have to be concerned about his ball or the ball he strikes ricocheting into, and displacing, your initial point. Let's say your ball is 18 inches in front, and they close in to 15 inches left of the pallino. A successful hit on their ball will not interfere with the position of your initial point.

When pointing, we recommend the smooth release generating the 12 o'clock to 6 o'clock rotation that we discussed in chapter 4. Make it your goal to place your initial point so close to pallino that your opponent needs two, three, or even four balls to beat it.

Subsequent Rolls

"Go to school" on subsequent rolls by you, your teammates or your opponents. Don't wander off, physically or mentally. Don't think about your next shot. Pay attention and read the path of the shots that every player takes in your game. Does a ball fall in a certain direction? How does a player adjust to a bad roll? Does the adjustment work? Does the player hit the sideboard too early or too late on a bank shot? Where do players stand when making a delivery – what angles do they get? Is the angle advantageous, or would another approach be better?

Moving the Pallino To Gain Advantage

There is a version of bocce that uses a large washer as the target. The object of the game is the same – score points by directing balls closer to the target than your opponent can. The difference, of course, is that the target will remain stationary. Its place at the start of the frame will be its position at the end of the frame. But in more conventional bocce using a pallino as the target, attempting to relocate the target ball adds another dimension of strategy. Since the position of the pallino may change at any time during a frame, players need to stay mindful of this. This should be both an offensive and defensive mindset. You need to consider "Where can I redirect the pallino to gain advantage?" and "Where might my opponent try to send the pallino, and how can I prevent or minimize my disadvantage?" Often this simply means keeping a ball near the endboard to prevent the other team from scoring easy points by knocking the object ball there.

"Reading The Green"

In the same area of the court, if a rolling ball falls or breaks to the left from one end, chances are it will fall to the right from the other end. A good player needs to accurately read this break and make adjustments.

When a ball falls or breaks in one direction, players tend to compensate for the break on subsequent shots. Instead of aiming at the target, they sight on a spot that, provided they get the same amount of break, will bring their ball into scoring position. This may or may not be successful. The court surface may crown or peak, and compensating by changing your aim on the next ball may surprise you. You may find it breaking in the opposite direction because it fell off the other side of the crown. For example, you take a smooth roll for point but the ball breaks twelve inches to the right preventing you from closing in for the point. You aim your next shot twelve inches farther to the left, hoping to curve this ball in to the pallino. To your surprise, this time the ball falls off to the left, still leaving your opponent with the nearest ball. When a ball's glide path is near the crown of a court surface, the direction of fall might be unpredictable. The best strategy: when a ball falls in one direction, players must adjust their position on the foul line. Move in the direction that the ball falls. Use the same glide path as on the previous shot, changing only your initial delivery point. If the ball falls right, move your body a step or two to the right. If the ball falls left, move to the left. This is the safest, most consistent strategy. The alternative, staying in the same position but changing the ball's path, can be effective if you have *court knowledge* (experience on the court's surface).

Taking A Chance Vs. Playing Safe

There is an element of risk in many shots that you take in a bocce game. For example, if you attempt a raffa and hit your own ball by mistake, you may help your opponent. If you play it safe, and try to outlag your opponent's ball, you may not score, but you minimize the damage. Which is the better option? That is a great question, and one for which I have a great answer. It depends. A player needs to take into consideration a host of factors. The score and the situation are critical to making a sound decision on strategy. When you are ahead and cruising toward a sure victory, you tend to get aggressive and "go for it." Behind in the score, and hoping to sneak back into the game might call for a more conservative approach. Late in the game consider – if successful, will this one daring play win the game? Has your opponent been surging in the last few frames? If the game goes to another frame, is the other team likely to take the victory? In the end, trust your instincts, make the play and, successful or not, don't second guess yourself. Trust that you made an intelligent decision based on the evidence you had at the time.

There always seem to be contradictory opinions on any piece of bocce strategy. It has taken me a long time, but I have finally discovered how to best evaluate the effectiveness of strategy. Wait until after the shot is taken – if it worked, it was good strategy, otherwise it was bad.

Don't be like our Massachusetts drivers who drive the same way no matter what the road conditions. Every weekday morning that we get some winter snow or slippery road conditions, there are commuters in fender benders all the way to Boston. Drive more cautiously when conditions warrant it. Play more aggressively when conditions are right, and more cautiously when the situation calls for it. Don't end up road kill on the bocce court.

"Selling" the Point

Sometimes a shot doesn't turn out the way a player intended. Instead of coming in for a point, the shot bumps an opponent's ball into scoring position, or knocks his own team's point out of contention. It may even move the pallino toward the opponent's ball(s) giving him the point(s). This is "selling" the point, a colorful phrase that depicts one of the most disheartening happenings in the game of bocce. You've become a "salesman" (or "salesperson" for the politically correct). If you play enough, it will happen to you. Deal with it.

Taking A Stand

One kind of tactical bocce is often overlooked. Players often give little thought to selecting the best starting position for an approach or delivery. A 10- or 12-foot court gives you a lot of options. You can legally start your approach anywhere along that 10- or 12-foot width. Walk along that line and check out the view. How much of the pallino do you see from different positions? Play the shot in your mind from the different angles and select the position that gives you the best percentage of being successful. Imagine that the shot ends up exactly as you hope it will. What will your opponents' options be then? Think ahead, then execute.

Sometimes moving to one side of the foul line or another opens up the target zone. For example, in some cases it may be advantageous to knock away your opponent's ball or the pallino. Since you aren't too concerned with which one you hit, move along the foul line to find the launch site that affords you the widest target zone. Whenever you are considering hitting, take into consideration the positions of any balls around your target. What is likely to happen if your shot is off and it hits one of them? How much risk is involved?

In this hit attempt, the player moves well to his right to get the best angle

Tactical Bocce – Blocking

Many players like to close off the opponents' angle by leaving a ball short of the pallino, or strategically placing a ball to make their attempt more difficult. This concept of blocking an opponent is really playing defense. "Put some pants on it," say shuffleboard players, encouraging a teammate to place a protective block on a well-positioned point. Sometimes a block is used to concede a point, while preventing the opposition from scoring multiple points. Often, players opt for laying their last ball in front. It blocks. It defends. It has nuisance value. It gives the opposition something to think about, and often limits their options.

A good defensive mindset is to concentrate on never allowing your opponents to score multiple points in a frame. A big score by the opposition boosts their confidence and puts added pressure on your team. Stay in the game by avoiding giving up two-, three- and four-point rounds.

Hit Early, Point Late

If you are debating whether to close in for point or hit your opponent's ball away, consider the following. If you are going to hit, do it first. Your point attempt might be short, and could possibly block your path to the target on subsequent attempts. Like billiards, you want to "see" the object in order to hit it. So hit early, point late. If you miss with the raffa or volo attempt, you can then decide to close in or try another hit. Teams may try to hit twice in a row, but usually not three times. If it is 11 o'clock (one point away from defeat in a twelve-point game) a team may try a third consecutive knockaway shot to save the game.

Consider this scenario: in a doubles match your opponents roll the pallino out and then place a close point requiring your team to hit. Your hit attempt misses and you decide to try a second hit. You might be inclined to say to your teammate, "Why don't you try it this time?" But the percentages are better if the same person attempts both hits. He can adjust by analyzing just how he missed the first try and, should he miss again, his teammate will have two chances to "close in" and "minimize the damage." This is better than two players each having one ball to lag.

Many good players like to hit an opponent's ball away, even if it isn't extremely close. As we pointed out in Chapter 5, players want to have a ball near the backboard as a kind of insurance against the pallino being knocked there later in the game. So, the knockaway shot presents a win-win situation. It serves its team well either by hitting its target, or rolling to the backboard.

When your team has three balls to play and your opponent has but one, hitting is a good option. For example, you establish the initial point with a roll 10 inches from the object ball. Your opponents try to hit your ball away and miss. They attempt to hit again and miss. Next they point and close in to eight inches from the pallino. They have one ball left, you have three. Since they are in, it is your turn. Hitting is a good option in this situation, even if you feel you can close in, because you want their ball out of there. If it stays, it's going to be a nuisance, perhaps even preventing you from scoring big. If you miss, you still have two balls to try to close in for point or hit (you make the call!).

Not Only What, But Who?

An important strategic consideration is not only what strategy to attempt, but which player should execute the task. You might consider who is more skilled at the particular type of shot, and who feels more confident about getting the job done. Another consideration is how many balls are left for each player to roll. For example, your team has three balls left to play, the other team has none. Your opponents are in for one point. You decide to hit. One player on your team has two balls to roll, and the other has one. The player with one ball left should attempt the hit. If he misses, his partner will still have two chances to close in for point. If he is short or long on the first attempt, he can adjust with the second ball and should win the frame. Had the player with two bocce balls attempted the hit and failed, he and his partner would then each have one chance to close in. The percentages, however, favor one player with two chances over two players with one chance each.

The Polaroid Approach & Positive Mental Imaging

In chapter 4, we introduced what I'll call the Polaroid approach. Stand near the backboard and take a mental Polaroid, pause to let it come into focus, then block everything out and focus on the shot. Before executing, create a positive mental image of a well-placed shot. Get your teammates to avoid comments that create a negative image. "Don't be short of the pallino" gives an image of a shot that doesn't quite reach its intended destination. "Make it reach beyond the pallino" creates a different picture in the mind. The body aspires to the mental images it processes. We teach our baseball players not to say things like "Don't lose 'em!" when the pitcher gets behind in the count. We want to hear encouragement that produces positive images. "Throw strikes, big guy!" or "Toss it right down the middle of the plate like you can, Mark!" are what we want to hear and they create the images we want to visualize.

There is a great deal of documentation supporting mental imagery as a valid tool for improving skills in basketball, football, swimming, karate, skiing, volleyball, tennis and golf. There is no reason it can't help your bocce. When attempting a roll with the game on the line, consider this three-step approach (with thanks to Dr. Cordano).

1. Take a deep breath.
2. Visualize the best shot you ever made.
3. Execute the shot with confidence.

Learning From Mistakes

True story – tournament blunder - the names have been changed to protect the inept.

My team was ahead 9-4 against what was arguably the best team in the tournament. They had just defeated another strong team, and it looked like the winner of our match would be the favorite in the finals.

In the next frame our opponents made a skillful hit that gave them three points. This buoyed them and they went on a run, taking the lead 11-9. In what would be the final frame, after rolling all four of their balls, they held the 12th and game-winning point, but we had two more rolls.

The pallino was about 2 feet off the sideboard and their point ball was about 2 feet in front of it and on the rail. We had a ball just in front of their ball (see photos).

The tournament rules allow for players to meet at half court to discuss strategy (four player teams – two stationed at each end). I met with my teammates Steve and Bob, and gave the following advice.

"Bob, if you hit our green ball, it will knock their red ball out and we will have two points. Then Steve can easily come in for the final point and we will win the game 12-11."

*We wanted to hit our green ball
causing the opponent's red ball to
deflect out of contention (The ball
closer to the pallino is the other team's
red, the ball behind it is our green)*

Bob made a good shot, but too soft. It hit our ball as it was supposed to, and knocked the point ball up like it was supposed to, but not far enough to take it out of contention.

*A too soft hit pushed the point
ball up, but it still held the point*

So Steve rolled the final ball… "Harder" I told him." He did the same thing – moving the balls, but not enough.

*A second soft hit pushed the
point a bit more, but not enough*

The problem was poor communication. When I was taking about hitting, they were thinking about nudging – they are both good pointers – the court was playing fast and they visualized a gentle hit that would do the job. Also, from their vantage point, it looked like the point ball was about even with the pallino, when in fact it was a couple feet short.

*A strong hit would have
produced this result and we
could then come in for the game
winner on the last ball*

Here's what we learned. When strategizing, you have to not only suggest what shot to make, but also how much speed it requires. Compounding matters was that, although the court was playing very fast, there was loose material where these balls were sitting. That slowed them down after they were struck.

The legendary LSU baseball coach Skip Bertman is fond of saying "A winner accepts responsibility for everything that happens to him. A loser points the finger at everybody else."

I messed up big time. If I were a good coach, I'd have said assertively and confidently, "The red ball is a couple feet short of the pallino and there is a lot of loose material there - we need a strong hit on our ball - I want their red ball to go to the backboard!" (A visual and vigorous pointing motion toward the backboard would have been in order).

Coach Bertman, it was my mistake, and it won't happen again!

Bocce – Simple Yet Elegant

Bocce is such a simple but elegant endeavor. On the surface it seems so elementary. Yet, as we have seen, it can involve sophisticated strategy and mental skills. Marco Cignarale is one of the growing breed of young and talented bocce players. He played the conventional games of basketball and soccer in high school, and learned bocce in his dad's backyard court. At the age of fifteen, he took second place at the World Series of Bocce in Rome, New York, spending his $500.00 cash prize on a new stereo. Cignarale sums the game up nicely. "It's really a mind game," says Marco. "One little mistake and you're done!"

Some Simple Strategic Suggestions

Drawing 1

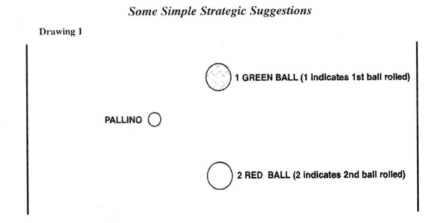

Some Simple Strategic Suggestions

Drawing 1

1 GREEN BALL (1 indicates 1st ball rolled)

PALLINO

2 RED BALL (2 indicates 2nd ball rolled)

After green made the initial point, red tried to outlag or outpoint figuring that if he didn't close in he would "spock" (hit) on his next attempt. However, the roll was short, blocking his angle to hit the green point. So, a better strategy is to hit first and point next. Hit, miss and point is preferable to point, miss and hit.

Drawing 2

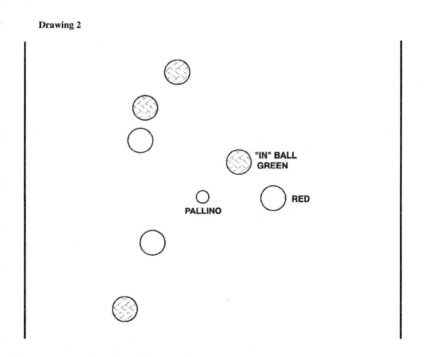

Drawing 2

On the last ball, should red try to hit the green point and try for three or four points? If he misses and hits the red, then green gets a point. If he inadvertently hits the pallino to the backboard, green may score multiple points. Let the score, the situation, and the player's skill influence the decision.

Drawing 3

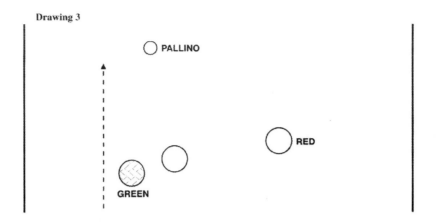

Drawing 3

If green elects to roll for point, he should aim to the left of the pallino because this offers two positive options:

1) The ball may close in for point to the left of the pallino.
2) The ball may tap the green ball into scoring position.

Drawing 4

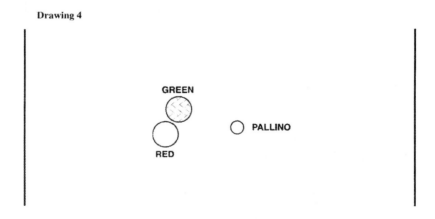

Drawing 4

Red's next shot should be a strong roll since if it taps the red ball already played, it will carom into the green and knock it out of contention (leaving red with the possibility of two points).

Drawing 5

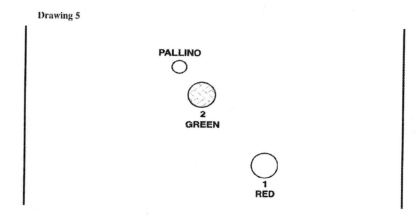

Drawing 5

Red rolls first and makes a good point. Green rolls next and outpoints red. Red decides to hit. Red should make the approach and delivery from the left side of the court to open up the widest target zone. The pallino may be knocked to the backboard from this angle or the green point may be hit away – both are positive outcomes for red (if the pallino is hit to the backboard, chances are the red ball will follow it).

Drawing 6

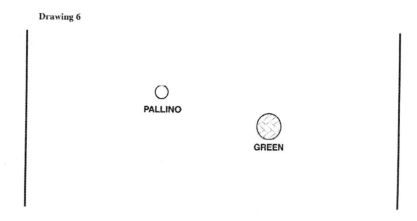

Drawing 6

Red thinks he can outpoint green's shot but hits anyway because he knows that a miss will leave a red ball at the endboard as insurance against the opponents knocking the pallino there later in the frame. This is a common strategy in areas where the backboard is played "live."

137

Drawing 7

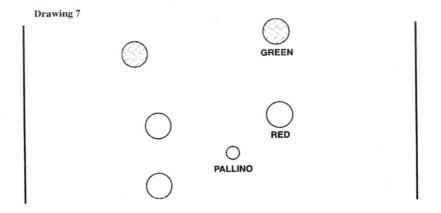

If you find yourself in the same position as the green team, you may want to make a strong roll at the pallino hoping to take it to the backboard for a possible two or three points.

Drawing 8

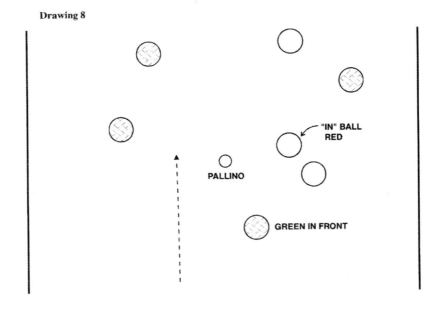

On red's last ball, stay left of the pallino – don't take a chance on hitting the green in front and "selling the point."

Drawing 9

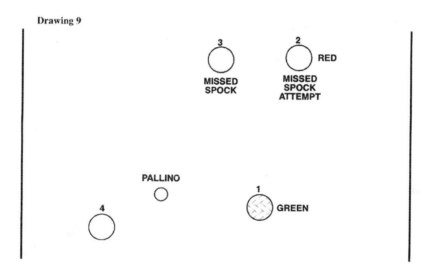

Drawing 9

Green rolled initial point. Red missed two hit attempts, then closed in for point. Green has three balls left to red's one. Hit in this situation.

Drawing 10

Drawing 10

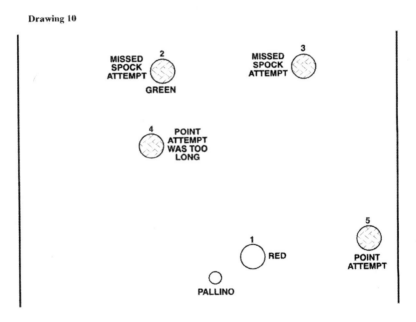

Green used all four balls and failed to take out or outpoint red's initial point. Red should stand to the left side of the court and roll off the right sideboard. If not rolled too hard, the red ball should knock green #5 out and stay in for a point. The same type shot executed softly two more times should score four points for red. These are relatively easy shots and make for a better percentage shot than trying to outpoint #5.

Drawing 11

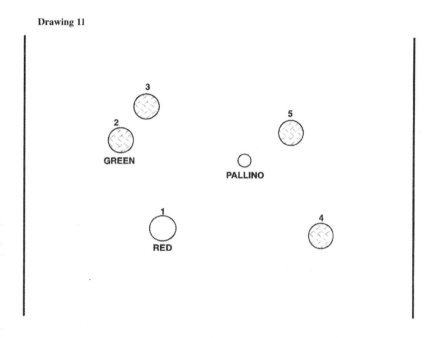

Drawing 11

Green took four shots to outlag red's initial point. With three balls left, red can either hit green's point (#5) or take the pallino to the backboard. Either way should score multiple points.

Drawing 12

Drawing 12

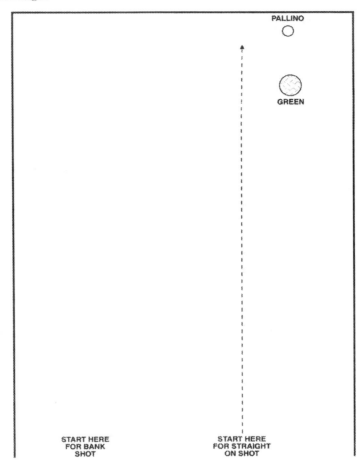

Green's point is short of the pallino and near the backboard. Red must decide whether to hit or point. If he elects to point there are two options:

1)roll straight on – aim left of pallino so as not to tap green closer, or
2)use bank shot.

Adjust your starting position accordingly.

Chapter 8
Building A Backyard Court

The following pages give step-by-step details for building a backyard court. To add insight to the process, photos and information are included chronicling the construction of my own family's court. Building my court served two purposes. It gave me the opportunity to advance to the next level of competition, and it gave me first-hand knowledge to better write this chapter on court construction. Comments concerning my backyard bocce court are separated from the text by a boxed outline.

You can have a great deal of enjoyment playing bocce without a professional-looking court on your premises, and thereby preserve your open space for other activities. One of the most attractive aspects of the sport has always been that it can be played by anyone almost anywhere. If you do opt for a court enclosed by sideboards and endboards, it is likely to be a permanent structure. The task of building a quality, permanent court is not to be taken lightly. To construct anything but the simplest of bocce courts, your yard is going to be in a state of disarray for weeks. Your lawn will likely be devastated by trucks delivering sand, gravel, stone dust or clay, and your relationship with significant others may be altered. You also need to consider the effect the court's construction will have on the neighborhood. Will it be a welcome sight or an eyesore? Is there a chance that you'll someday put up spotlights for night play? How will this affect the neighborhood's tranquility?

The Building Site

Once you've made the decision to build, spend some time deciding on its precise location. Side yard or backyard? Are there trees and shrubs that will have to be sacrificed? How does the land pitch from one end to the other? Where can you build that allows you to create the court that meets the dimensions you desire? Is one area more conducive to good drainage than another? Soil types and drainage patterns vary widely from one area to another (you can install perforated pipe to aid drainage). How will sunrise and sunset affect play? Some builders recommend that the court's length run north to south to prevent annoying glare at dawn and dusk.

The final site should be the rectangular piece of your property that comes closest to satisfying the above issues. You may have to make trade-offs. The most level area available to you may not be the most esthetically pleasing or the most convenient location for the alley. You may have to sacrifice or relocate favored trees or shrubs.

My family owns a home on a corner lot in a pleasant, family neighborhood. We debated the merits of building the court on our side yard (surrounded by a four-foot tall, split picket fence) vs. our backyard (enclosed by a six-foot chain link fence). We finally opted for the privacy afforded by the backyard, which also preserved our side yard's open space for other activities like wiffle ball, badminton, and bocce on the lawn. I had hoped for a 76- by 12-foot court, but settled for 76 by 10 because I wasn't willing to sacrifice a row of fruit trees that border the playing area. The compromise worked well as the line of trees gives a European ambiance to our court.

The Dimensions

People always ask if a court is regulation or "official" size. The question is difficult to answer because different governing bodies mandate different court dimensions. Here on the East Coast there are many 12 by 60 foot courts, built to International Bocce Association standards, (a group that is now defunct). However, organizations in other areas prefer larger courts of 70 to 90 feet in length. True international court dimensions are 27.5 by 4 meters for volo play, and 26.5 by 3.8 to 4.5 for punto, raffa, volo competition. (We discuss these styles of play in Chapter 12, International Play). So, if you want a court that meets these specifications, you'll want one that is approximately 90 feet long by 13 feet wide.

You can build a court of any length and width that you desire, unless you plan to host a tournament. That tournament court will have to meet the specifications outlined in the governing body's rules. As we have stated, there are courts as short as 60 feet and as long as 90 feet or more. Widths run anywhere from eight feet to 14 feet or more. Another thing to factor into your decision is the cost. The bigger the court, the greater the cost for materials and construction (also, the greater the effort and expense to maintain).

How Long?

Many veteran players don't like the 60-foot courts, maintaining that they are too short and provide too small a playing area. Many rules require the initial toss of pallino to come to rest on or beyond the half court marker (30 feet). Since a player may hit or spock from the 10-foot line, a target near midcourt may be as close as twenty feet away. Compounding the problem is that in many local tournaments, players get away with flagrantly violating the foul line. Their approach and delivery bring them practically on top of the ball they're trying to hit. Many bocce players prefer longer courts (in the 70 to 76 foot range). This seems a good compromise between the 60 and 90 foot extremes. You have enough open court to make for challenging play, and the size is reasonable for a family's backyard.

How Wide?

Courts are as narrow as eight feet (or less) and as wide as 14 (or more). Widening the court minimizes the luck factor and maximizes the need for skillful play. For example, picture a court eight feet wide with the pallino resting at one end right in the center of that width. Considering only the width, the worst possible shot a player could make will end up no more than about four feet to the left or right of the target. A wider court means more open space calling for more precise rolling. Ten to twelve feet is a reasonable width.

To make your decision on court dimensions, take all of the foregoing into consideration. Keep in mind the difference between a court for backyard, recreational use and one for league or international tournament play. If you want to represent your country in international play, construct the large court. Otherwise, build it to fit your situation, your yard, and your pocketbook. Most of all, build the court that makes you happy. If you only have room for a small court, fine! Build it and enjoy it. Don't let the court's size diminish the joy of playing. My good friend Del Bracci of Bradford, Massachusetts had only enough room on the side of his house for a 9' by 45' stone dust court. This "derringer" of a court has been nothing but a source of great enjoyment for Bracci and the host of players who compete there.

Another Trade-Off

Before we built our court, we played exclusively on our grassy, side yard and became pretty good players. When we entered tournaments played on stone dust or clay courts, however, we regularly got trounced. Several months after completing our court, my son James and I competed in a tournament in Old Lyme, Connecticut on 76- by 12-foot courts. We played pretty well, winning several matches and competing well in those that we lost. The backyard court is clearly helping us get to the next level. But it's somewhat disturbing that we don't seem to play on the lawn any more. Lawn bocce is a wonderful game full of challenging natural obstacles.

While in Connecticut for the above-mentioned tournament, we visited friends from the 1995 Special Olympics Bocce Committee at the home of Roger Lord. After a delightful cook-out and reunion, we played lawn bocce. Roger has a world-class bocce lawn. The course has rolling hills and level areas and is a delight to play on. You need to be able to roll oh, so gently downhill and sometimes you have to heave the ball volo-like uphill. And you have to read the green like a golfer on the PGA tour. I had almost forgotten how much joy good friends and good lawn bocce could provide. Building a backyard court brings with it this trade-off. You are going to get better at competitive tournament-style bocce, but you are probably not going to play much on the lawn again.

Initial Grading

Once you have the site and court dimensions selected, stake out the area using wooden stakes and mason's line. The staked area should be slightly larger than the finished playing area to allow access for heavy equipment. You'll need to strip the entire area of sod and loam, probably digging up and removing 12 inches of material. Grading with a bulldozer, Bobcat, or front-end loader may be necessary. The final playing surface must be as level as possible to provide for the best possible playing conditions. Some suggest treating the stripped area with herbicide or putting down rolls of plastic landscape fabric to prevent new growth of grass or weeds coming up through the court surface. Let your environmental conscience be your guide in this matter.

Sideboards, Squaring The Court, Leveling The Boards

Once the playing area is stripped, reset the stakes to the precise play area measurements. Put up the sideboards now, using a transit, carpenter's level, or line level. Leaving one endboard until last allows for easy access for a wheelbarrow or machinery to deliver and spread materials. The side and endboards may be of any material that will not move when struck by a ball. They must be at least as high as the balls (6 to 12 inches recommended). Both

The different phases of court construction

ends should be higher to protect spectators and players because most balls knocked out of the court exit near the ends. You can construct the court walls with landscaping timbers (6" x 6" or 8" x 8"), or wood planking. Pressure treated stock is highly recommended. Note: Some courts are built with concrete around the perimeter and then lined on the inside with pressure treated wood. According to the United States Bocce Federation, this promotes "billiard-like accuracy for balls rebounding off the side walls." Be sure to square the ends of the boards before installing them. To square the court, measure the diagonal distance between corner stakes. The lengths should be equal. Use a transit to mark the stakes at the appropriate height and secure the line tightly at these marks. For example, if you are using 12-inch high sideboards, mark one stake 12 inches from the subsurface and shoot your transit readings from that mark. Without a transit, use the longest level you can obtain and, instead of marking the stakes, set one sideboard in place at a time using the mason line and leveling as you go along. Remember, save one of the endboards for last. Set the other side of the court along the mason's line, leveling it relative to the first side. Use a board long enough to reach across the width of the court for this job, reading the carpenter's level that is placed on top. Drive stakes two to three feet into the ground to shore up the boards and keep them straight. Use the mason's line to guide your work on the sideboards.

Some builders recommend steel reinforcing rods 5/8" in diameter by 24" long if the side walls are three inches or thicker. The idea is to drill holes vertically down through the width of the boards every five or six feet, driving the rods into the ground until they are flush with the top of boards. With two-inch or narrower boards you can use 1" x 24" rods. Drive these into the ground against the sideboards at five- to six-foot intervals and attach with u-bolt clamps. Use no reinforcing rods in the endboards since they experience the most wear and tear and are the most likely to need repair or replacement. Also, be aware that steel rods used externally will eventually rust.

Note: You may want to drill a small hole through the endboard to allow excessive water to drain after rainstorms. Drill the hole parallel to, and just above the court's surface. This is important if you are running a tournament, and don't have time to wait for your court to dry out naturally.

The bocce court surface

The leveling process

After much deliberation, we decided to situate our court in the backyard between our chain link fence and row of apple and pear trees. We could attach the sideboards on one side to the existing fence posts. The court would have the chain-link fence on one side, and an attractive row of fruit trees on the other. One of the first problems we encountered was a 20-inch drop in elevation from one end of our proposed play area to the other. We shot a line with a transit and put up the sideboards as level as possible. We decided on pressure treated planking, using 2" x 12" x 16' boards. Setting five boards end to end on each side would give us an eighty foot court that we could later cut back to 76 feet. We used the existing chain-link fence posts as stakes, attaching the boards to them with a post-to-fence bracket. The brackets were screwed into the sideboard with 1 1/2" galvanized decking screws and then fastened to the pipe with the hardware packaged with the bracket. On the opposite side of the court we drove galvanized steel pipes into the ground with a heavy sledge hammer and fastened the brackets around these and onto the sideboards. We used metal tie plates to align the joints of two abutting planks (top and bottom).

Hats off to my good friend and handyman, Joe Austin, who served as foreman and chief laborer on the job. Heck, the guy installed his own in-ground pool--I figured I could trust my bocce court to him.

With the sides up and the grass and loam removed, we went about bringing in the sub-surface materials.

The Sub-Surface Materials

We recommend a five-inch layer of sand followed by three inches of crushed stone. This will ensure good drainage. Many builders skip the sand and use only gravel or crushed stone as a base. Other than #1 or #2 crushed stone, a gravel mix, or any mixture of pebbles, ground shell, sand, or soil that provides adequate drainage may be used. The USBF recommends three inches of baserock (two inches in diameter) to avoid the risk of gravel or smaller stone ultimately working its way to the surface and creating a rough course. Some builders recommend wetting and compacting the subsurface with a tamper or a gas-driven compactor. Others opt for doing the compacting only when the final surface is in place.

> For this work we hired a contractor who used a front-end loader to spread and level the materials. We then screwed and/or toe nailed 10-foot two-by-fours across the width of the court at the bottom of the sideboards. These two-by-fours, buried under the surface material, help reinforce the consistent 10-foot width of our court.

Choosing The Surface Material

A Tale Of Three Popular Choices (Stone Dust, Oyster Shell, Clay)

{With input from Tom McNutt, Michael Grasser, and David Brewer, the three top names in the American bocce court building business.}

Although people use all sorts of different bocce surface materials (grass, indoor/outdoor carpet, Astroturf), the following three come up most often in court construction conversations. Stone dust, crushed oyster shell, and clay are the "Cadillacs" of surface materials.

According to bocce court builder Tom McNutt (boccemon.com), they are the only materials that give you the ability to level the court, maintain it without undue effort, and produce an acceptable "speed to bounce ratio." We want speed but we don't want bounce. If we rated materials on a scale of one to ten, with ten being the optimal score, concrete might score a 10 for speed and a 0 for bounce (it plays fast – that's good, hence 10 - but provides a pretty hefty bounce on a volo attempt – that's bad, hence 0). At the other end of the spectrum we might find that sand scores a 0 for speed and a 10 for bounce (ball doesn't roll so fast, but won't bounce).

Stone dust, oyster shell, and clay produce very acceptable speed/bounce numbers.

Stone Dust

Stone dust is popular because of its exceptional drainage qualities and low cost. It is especially appropriate in New England (where it is easily obtained) and in places that get lots of rain. In some areas, stone dust is known as decomposed granite. On the west coast, builders refer to it as "quarter stone by dust." Most stone dust is actually crushed limestone. Bocce court builder and Michigan landscape architect Mike Grasser prefers crushed limestone, sometimes mixing two or three parts with one part clay for the top 1/8-inch court surface.

Grasser also has considerable expertise with artificial surfaces, having traveled extensively in Europe interviewing synthetic bocce court product specialists. "If you opt for carpet," he warns, "check the nap." If carpet fibers don't stand up straight (are not at right angles to the floor), a court is likely to roll faster in one direction than the other. Astroturf surfaces are preferable in this regard, as the fibers tends to be short and sturdy.

As far as high end synthetics go, Grasser has experience with surfaces that roll out like linoleum. Most, he maintains, tend to crack or split after a couple years of play. Carpets tend to stretch too, leaving wrinkles and "waves" after a season or two. The best artificial surfaces are poured, self-leveling substances which are popular in European bocce facilities. Developed for indoor, covered courts, the surface can be used outdoors in climates that don't experience frost. Such courts usually include "channel drains" around the perimeter to sweep out surface puddles after rainstorms. As you might expect, these maintenance-free courts are among the most expensive on the market.

Crushed Oyster Shell

The shell of the oyster is very popular on the West Coast where it is readily available. The oyster beds of San Francisco Bay are a popular source. Primarily used to create agricultural by-products for soil fertilization as well as chicken and cattle feed enhancers, oyster shell makes an excellent bocce surface. Tom McNutt prefers this top dressing, and begins with a base of crushed Pacific oyster shell (same stuff you would get by grinding up your oysters on the half shell). These are ¾" and smaller.

Next comes a layer of finer oyster flakes. Finally the court is topped off with very fine oyster flour (a powder used as a soil amendment – farmers or gardeners might use it to return calcium to the soil). McNutt reports that his oyster shell courts are playable even shortly after heavy rains.

Note: Some court builders prefer to mix the oyster shell with clay or crusher fines.

Clay (Har-Tru, Baseball Infield/Warning Track Clay)

Although some bocce court builders use baseball infield clay or warning track clay as a topping, the most appropriate "clay" is really not a clay. Manufactured by Lee Tennis, Har-Tru is sometimes called "American clay" – it's actually crushed metabasalt (very hard, angular volcanic stone). According to New England sales representative Pat Hannsen, "Har-Tru performs better than clay because clay absorbs water and holds it, making the surface unplayable rapidly, while drying out slowly." Har-Tru's product includes gypsum which acts as an initial set-up aid. Once cured, the product plays well and allows excess water to drain by percolating down through the medium.

Har-Tru plays fast and true and has excellent speed/bounce numbers when installed correctly. I put one inch of this product over my stone dust court to "step up" to a faster playing surface. I was a little concerned about drainage, but once it "cured" or "set", it drained quite well (had a heavy rainfall on a Sunday and was able to play our regular Monday morning league as usual).

For a free, no obligation quote on Har-Tru material for your court, visit joyofbocce.com and fill out the Quote Request Form available via the navigation button labeled Har-Tru.

David Brewer of BocceBrew.com tells me...

"We read your book years ago and it was an inspiration to investigate court design and construction. We have built 65 courts in the last three and a half years, including courts for John Madden, George Lucas, headquarters for Yahoo.com, wineries, hotels, restaurants, public parks, retirement communities and private homes."

Like his Pacific Northwest counterpart, Tom McNutt, Brewer favors the readily available oyster shell, using it in a one-to-one mixture with infield clay. "It is very malleable," says Brewer, "making the courts easy to level and maintain." Running a drag brush or broom over the surface makes for quick and easy grooming between games. Water percolates well through oyster shell, and the surface will harden, but not as much as stone dust or Har-Tru. All of the above, combined with the fact that crushed limestone is virtually unavailable on the West Coast, makes oyster shell an outstanding choice.

George C. Scott, playing the boxer's father in the 1979 movie Rocky Marciano, proclaims that "In Italia, a rich man's bocce court – a real bocce court – is made of the crushed shell from the oyster."

The Big Three
in Bocce Court Construction
Contact David Brewer at www.boccebrew.com (415-461-8842)
Contact Michael Grasser at 248-681-9022
Contact Tom McNutt at www.boccemon.com (360-224-2909).

The Surface

Finally, after deciding on your surface, spread up to three inches of the material. Another option is to put a one-inch top coat of your material of choice over your existing surface. If you opt for the one-inch topping, some recommend putting it down in four applications of 1/4 inch at a time. Wet and roll the material with a heavy roller between applications. The surface must be dry enough that it doesn't collect on the roller during this process.

We added three inches of stone dust, again using the heavy machinery to deliver and level the material. We wet and rolled the surface with a heavy roller, repeating the process daily. Playing games in between helps expose the high and low spots. An option is to let the surface settle for a season and then add an inch of either brick dust or fine sifted clay, or Har-Tru top dressing (caution - these may be tracked into the house). I opted for one inch of Har-Tru after a couple years of play, and am very happy with the choice. Plays fast and true – drains well, but not as well as stone dust – cures very hard so that weeds can't take root – drawback = once New England fall weather sets in (freezing and thawing season) we have to shut down until the spring. Water gets locked up as ice in the morning, then melts and surface becomes soggy as sun rises and temperature increases.

Leveling The Surface

Roll the surface with a heavy roller. Wet the surface down, let it dry, and roll again. After the initial rolling process, use an angle iron or a straight board about the width of the court and drag it lengthwise across the court. This scraping process, called screeding by concrete workers, removes high spots and fills in low points. Repeat this screeding process several times, wetting and rolling between each pass. You can also use a rigid rake 36 inches or more in width to scrape and grade the surface. These are sometimes called infield rakes because baseball groundskeepers use them. They have teeth on one side, and a grading surface on the other (see photo of lute/scarifier).

Leveling the final surface takes some time and help from Mother Nature in the form of rainfall. A good soaking rainstorm speeds up the leveling process considerably by exposing low spots (puddles) that you can fill with additional

material. A galvanized fence post the width of the court can also help with leveling. Set it down across the width of the court and place a four-foot carpenter's level on top of it. (See photo) Besides the feedback from the bubble in the level, low spots and irregularities show up clearly when light passes underneath the bar.

157

Initially, the surface will be soft enough so that a ball dropped from waist level or above will leave an indentation where it strikes the ground. Over time the surface should get harder and play faster. Volo shots that strike the surface will leave large, round indentations at first. As the court surface becomes harder, the size of the indentation will get smaller. These marks may start out the size of a softball on a new court. Eventually, they shrink to the size of a silver dollar, half dollar, and then a quarter. When they approximate the size of a dime, the court is fully settled.

Swingboard Construction

Use two-by-tens slightly shorter than the court's width as swingboards. At each end of the court, suspend the boards just off the court surface using screw hooks that latch onto eye bolts inserted into the backboard. During play, these swingboards absorb the energy of raffa impacts, thus discouraging rebound attempts off the endboard. Usually, builders cover this board with a material (carpet, rubber, old fire hose) that adds to the "give" of the board and protects it from damage. Other backboard designs are acceptable, but it is essential to have backboards constructed in such a way that they allow only minimal (or no) bounce back.

Swingboards must minimize bounce back

Extra height at the ends of the court help ensure balls stay in the court

Extra Height At The Ends

To ensure that balls hit by raffa and volo attempts stay in the court, you will need additional height at the endboards and sideboards near both ends. You can accomplish this by adding additional tiers or levels of boards. Fasten these boards securely to the existing structure and brace them with wood stakes and/or metal brackets. Use galvanized screws, not nails. You will have to gauge how far out from the endboard to extend this added height (16 feet recommended).Some recommend courts with an interesting staircase effect. The sideboards are one foot high. Starting at 12 feet from the endboard the height of the sides increases to three, four, then five feet high. (See photo below.) This increases the cost of construction and might be overkill unless you play with very

*Staircase construction - Szot Park,
Chicopee, Massachusetts*

hard rolling hitters. Also, spectators often struggle to see over the fortress-like planking.

> We added a second tier of two-by-twelves to each end of our court. These extended 16 feet from each end. We fastened them with metal brackets and wood strips (see photo previous page). We covered the swingboards with old fire hose donated by our local fire department.

Tools And Materials Needed

landscaping timbers or planking for side and endboards (pressure treated)
steel reinforcing rods or other means for staking boards
sand
crushed stone
surface material (clay, stone dust, or other screened topping)
heavy machinery (backhoe, Bobcat, etc.)
pick
shovel
rake
hammer
sledge hammer
ax (for tree or root removal)
transit
four foot or longer carpenter's level
line level
mason's line
framing square
100-foot steel tape measure
heavy lawn roller
L-shaped framing brackets and metal tie plates
screws (not nails) 1½- and 3-inch galvanized decking screws
9- or 12-volt battery operated screw gun AC/DC
circular saw

Court Markings

Depending on whose rules you intend to play by, your court markings will be different. Some groups play with one foul line that is both for pointing and hitting. I recommend this unless you aspire to play international rules. On those long courts they use one line for pointing, another for raffa hitting, and a third for volo hitting (the hitting shots require a longer runway). Many 60-foot courts utilize a foul line for pointing four feet from each backboard, and a foul line for hitting 10 feet from each backboard. Hopefully, as the game continues to grow, a standard will emerge that will be embraced by all the various groups. At any rate, the lines are generally painted on both side boards. (See photo page 37) You may also want to (especially for tournament play) put down a chalk line on the surface much like a baseball foul line.

For international play, the pointing and raffa line is four meters from the endboard, while the volo line is seven meters from the end. See Chapter 12 for international rules and contact the United States Bocce Federation (see chapter 6) for additional information on international courts and tournament play.

Most rules call for the initial toss of the pallino to come to rest at or beyond midcourt. You will need to paint this line on both sideboards as well. Again, for league or tournament play you may want a chalk line running across the surface.

Finally, many rules call for the first toss of pallino to come to rest a minimum distance from the backboard (e.g. three or four feet from the backboard). The Open Rules outlined in chapter 11 are gaining momentum and they contain no such restriction except that the initial toss of pallino not touch the backboard.

I prefer one line for hitting and pointing and this works well on the larger 76-foot court. I opted for a 10-foot foul line.

Top Dressing Technique

When our bocce group top dressed my backyard court, we photographically chronicled the progress (see following photos). I already had a satisfactory surface of stone dust over crushed stone and sand. It played pretty well and drained beautifully (there could be a heavy downpour and a couple hours later my court was playable). Still, we wanted to "step up" to a faster surface like the top bocce players use.

After some research I opted for Har-Tru material, the popular tennis court surface that is making inroads into the bocce court market. I'd add a one-inch top coat of this over the existing stone dust. Somewhat concerned about drainage, the manufacturer and others who owned or played on such courts allayed my fears.

The good people at Lee Tennis in Virginia determined that I'd need about 5 tons of Har-Tru to create a one-inch top coat for my 76' by 10' court. A do-it-yourself project from the get-go, our bocce crew lifted, lugged, laid down, leveled, and landscaped 125 eighty-pound bags of Har-Tru. And it was one "L" of a job!

Materials needed:

Har-Tru or other top dressing material (manufacturer will calculate how much you need - get a few extra bags to have on hand for repairs)

one straight 2 by 4 for "screeding" (should be about 6 inches shorter than the width of the court)

four pieces of strapping (8 feet long or longer)

transit (and someone who knows how to use it)

level (at least 4 feet long)

shovels

rakes

tamper

wheelbarrow

garden hose or two

heavy roller

one crew of workers (willing to work for food and/or beverages)

Procedure:

(The following assumes that we are starting with a relatively level surface over which we will place the top dressing.)

Place unopened bags of surface material onto or near one end of the court area. Lay two pieces of strapping (actual measurements 1½" by 1") down about one third of the distance from each side board (the eight-foot length running parallel to the length of the court).

Begin by placing strapping (these are 8 footers) at one end of court, leveling them using transit.

Set transit up (properly leveled) at opposite end and carefully level these pieces of strapping - getting a reference point that you can use consistently throughout the job. We placed a yard stick on end right atop the strapping and were able to sight on the stick's calibrations. You may have to dig material out from under the strapping or add more material beneath to level them. Verify the reference point at both ends of each piece of strapping.

Level the transit at the opposite end of the court.

Find someone who knows how to operate that transit.

Determine a reference point for leveling, and use this consistently as you work your way down the court.

Open bags and dump material onto the court starting at the end board and moving down the length of the strapping.

Open bags and dump top dressing onto court and over strapping.

Take the straight two-by-four and "screed" the material. Screeding is a masonry term for leveling concrete by dragging a straight object over it, pulling excess material away, and smoothing out the surface. It takes two people on their knees to maneuver the two-by-four. Use a side-to-side motion as you screed the material toward you – thus, the two-by-four must be about 6 inches shorter than the width of the court.

Begin the "screeding" process. Note: there is no grid here – those are morning shadows cast by our chain link fence.

Set another two pieces of strapping in place starting from the ends of the previously placed pieces. Level these properly and then carefully remove the first two pieces of strapping, filling in the spaces that they leave with new material.

A trowel can be used to smooth over any minor "bumps and bruises."

A trowel comes in handy for finish work.

Continue down the court in this manner…moving the strapping, checking the reference points, leveling, adding top dressing, screeding, and troweling. The person with the trowel may want to place a piece of plywood down to better bear his/her weight while doing the surface "finish work". Also, workers may opt for surgical masks while working in close proximity to the fine particulates of the top dressing.

Continue leveling and checking reference point with transit.   *Surgical masks for working with fine particulates.*

Continue down the court.

Carefully remove strapping and fill in the space with more material.

A good "finish man" is worth his weight in gold.

Once all the material is in place and leveled you must wet it thoroughly. ALL of the material must be wet. On subsequent wetting and rolling sessions, only the surface needs to be moist.

Use a garden hose to thoroughly wet all the material.

We used a Y connection added to our backyard faucet and got two hoses going at once. Periodically we took "coring samples" with the trowel to see if the bottom-most part of the material was getting wet. The idea is to make sure it is thoroughly wet but not drenched so that it becomes mush.

The material needs to be completely wet so that it can "cure" or "set up" over the next couple of days.

Next, roll with a heavy roller and use a tamper to get the edges and corners where the roller can't reach. Roll again each day as you wait for the material to "set."

The heavier the roller the better (600 lb. recommended).

A tamper comes in handy for corners and edges.

I knew that my Har-Tru bocce court top dressing would play fast and true. But an unexpected bonus is that, once it hardens sufficiently, it is virtually weed free. With my previous stone dust surface, we'd spend time between frames weeding the court (not a major problem, but a nuisance). The only weeds that can take root are around the perimeter (near the sideboards where the heavy roller can't quite reach). Use a tamper to address this problem.

Pat Hanssen of Lee Tennis gives us his take on the top dressing process...

"Once the screenings have been graded and compacted, the court is ready for the Har-Tru surface. Buy four (4) 1 1/4" O.D. steel pipes, 20' in length, and lay them along the two sides at the edge of the court. Get a long heavy board, cut it about 1/2" shorter than the width of the court and attach metal flashing at the ends. This board will slide easily across the pipes (attach two broom handles for easy handling) screeding out the Har-Tru surface to precisely 1 1/4" depth. Dump 10-12 bags in front of screed board, fluff up material with a rake or, lute/scarifier, and spread evenly across the front of the screed. As the board is pulled, one person can redistribute the Har-Tru as needed to fill in high and low spots. As material runs out, stop and open more bags until the process is complete.

When compacted dry, with a hand or power roller (500 - 1200 LBS of compaction preferred), 1" surface depth will have been achieved. Saturate thoroughly, allow the court to set up, and then roll again. Repeat until desired level of compaction is achieved."

Compactor

Some Interesting Options

You may want to consider spectator benches for your court. They should be placed carefully, considering both the fans' view of the game and their safety. Fewer balls fly out of the court near the center than at the ends, so caution dictates that they be placed accordingly. It is rarely seen today, but some bocce players install angle boards (45 degrees from each side to the endboard) that can be used for ricochet and carom shots. Others favor a bumper board over a swingboard. This bumper board doesn't swing, but acts as a shock absorber, collecting the energy of a fast moving ball. Still others use a ditch instead of an endboard. If your ball ends up in the ditch, it is dead. Finally, consider leaving a cut-out or removable section somewhere along your sideboards to allow for both handicap access as well as easy entry and exit for your heavy roller.

Synthetic courts may bring the game to yet another level. Not only is there almost no maintenance involved, but the game becomes very clean. I mean, your hands don't even get dirty. If synthetic surfaces (poured self-leveling surfaces, indoor/outdoor carpet, Astroturf) become the rage and the game flourishes the way aficionados think it will, the sport will likely welcome the designer clothes market.

Portable Courts

Free-standing (portable) courts represent still another option. These can be assembled in twenty minutes or so, played on, and then broken down for storage. Portable courts can be set up outdoors on a level patch of grass or earth, or indoors on composition floors like in a school gymnasium. They are used to conduct tournaments in hotels and convention halls. Courts are set up on the hotel carpet for example, with the carpet becoming the playing surface. After the tournament, the court is dismantled and the hotel has its hall or meeting room back.

My bocce group commissioned a tradesman to build a portable court of wood construction. It can be assembled by a several people in about twenty minutes using only ratchet sets. We set it up in our high school field house that has a poured rubber floor and use it for intramurals and for adult evening play in the winter. When finished playing, we disassemble it so that it doesn't interfere with physical education classes. We figure that bocce poses no threat to the composition floor since they heave the 16-pound shot there during track meets. We've even "sold" the physical education teachers on bocce as a class unit.

My bocce mates also fashion wooden temporary courts out of two-by-eights, setting them up on Astroturf at a place called Home Run Park in Lawrence, Massachusetts. An old mill building from Lawrence's heyday as a textile mill town, the place is now redesigned for baseball/softball practice areas. The problem was that our two-by-eights warped and not only looked bad, but made us play even worse than usual! So, we "bit the bullet" and forked over the money for thirty-three 6" by 6" timbers (8 feet long). We placed nine end to end and then three at each end to make two 12' by 72' courts. We set them up, play a couple hours, and dismantle and store them for the next time we play. Yes, they are a tad heavy, but we manage. Recently, we purchased another thirty-three timbers and now have 4 temporary courts.

8' timbers frame courts at Home Run
Park - Lawrence, MA

Canopies

After posting George Farruggio's photos (Punta Gorda, Florida courts with the canopy coverings) on my web site, I was inundated with questions about canopies. Joy of Bocce Weekly reader David Beacco was kind enough to send this valuable information.

"The canopies that cover the ends of those bocce courts are similar to ones for sale at our local Costco wholesale stores. They are 12 ft wide by 20 ft long for $179.00."
Beacco was kind enough to provide some links…

http://www.fstcinc.com/bc7.htm

http://www.angelfire.com/biz/shadecanopies/

http://www.aah-canopies.com/orkincan.html

http://tarps.com/econoretail.htm

I like the idea of the shade and protection from the elements that the canopies might provide (especially here in New England), but am wondering if it will curtail or alter our volo attempts…maybe forcing us to toss lower trajectory volos for fear of hitting the canopy.

Lighting

If you install lights for night play, they need to be high enough that they aren't shining directly in players' eyes. Also, in analyzing their placement you need to take into account what shadows are likely to be cast. Len Hickey of Wilbraham, Massachusetts has great lighting at his court on his business property – tall telephone poles with powerful lights shining down from high above. He has been petitioned to attach a bug zapper up by the lights to attract and electrocute those pesky mosquitoes. Len's lights are on a timer, and local high school kids hang out there and play bocce some evenings until the lights go out. Good, safe fun!

Court Maintenance

A well-constructed court should pose only a minimal maintenance problem. The court needs to be groomed after use by brooming, rugging (dragging a rug attached to a rope), or otherwise dragging the surface. The broom, rug, or other device used should be at least 24 inches wide. Thirty-six to 48 inches or more would be preferable to allow for the fewest number of passes when grooming. Fewer passes mean less work and fewer seams where material might collect. The 7-foot drag brush from Lee Tennis is easily the best bocce grooming tool (see chapter 6).

7' drag brush from Lee Tennis

Occasionally you will have to wet and roll the surface. This will be anywhere from once a month to once a week depending on how much use (and rain) your court gets. Be sure to examine the surface right after rainstorms and fill in any low spots. In the spring you may have to do an annual screeding and some realignment of the sideboards. Occasionally an endboard that has taken its share of raffas needs to be repaired or replaced.

If your court has level side boards and endboards you can make use of what is called a "screed board." Take a board almost as wide as the court and screw boards to each end so that you can sit the whole thing across the court's width. The boards screwed to the ends of the middle board rest on the sideboards of the court (see photo below). This puts the bottom of the middle board at the right height to "grade" the new, soft material to the "right height". Use a builder's level (or transit, or water level) to level these boards end to end and side to side.

Screed board

Court Construction Synopsis

1. Pick the site
2. Decide on dimensions
3. Stake out an area larger than the actual playing area using wooden stakes and mason's line
4. Strip the area of sod and dirt (12 inches)
5. Reset stakes to actual court dimensions
6. Put up sideboards using transit, carpenter's level, or line level, leaving one end board for last
7. Bring in and spread sub-surface materials
8. Bring in and spread surface materials
9. Compact and level surface using the screeding process, raking, wetting, and heavy roller
10. Add final end board and additional tiers for desired height
11. Install swingboard
12. Paint court markings
13. Revel in the outdoors and the joy of bocce

An Inexpensive Alternative
Backyard Bocce's Portable Courts

Backyard Bocce, Inc. has brought to market a line of portable bocce courts that are both practical and reasonably priced. Developer Chris Pfeiffer's concept grew out of his experience with Special Olympics, and a portion of the proceeds from sales benefit SO.

There are three different Backyard Bocce courts to choose from (all are 12' by 60'). Two of these courts are templates. They are portable, lightweight, and extremely easy to assemble and disassemble. The third court is enclosed with mesh sideboards.

The only pre-requisite for these courts is a reasonably level stretch of grass or dirt that measures about 12' by 60'. Set-up of the template courts is not unlike pitching a tent. You stretch out the template, pull it tight with bungee cords, then drive a couple of stakes into the ground. Next, plant some flags indicating end lines and half court (visual landmarks), and you are set to go within five minutes. Foul lines are demarcated by green and red vinyl sewn into the material ten feet from each end.

Although many of us like longer courts, most SO bocce is on 12' by 60' of real estate, and the decision to opt for these dimensions is probably a good one for backyard play.

You can choose from economical one-inch vinyl or two-inch vinyl templates.

These two products are more boundaries than they are courts. They simply demarcate a 12' by 60' rectangle for play. Any ball that rolls or is knocked out of the rectangle is out of play – a "dead ball."

The courts solve one nagging problem for lawn bocce players. They limit how far left or right a player may move to roll a ball. Sometimes a well played point is right in front of the object ball.

To avoid knocking it closer, the opponent gains a better angle by moving a step to the left, then another, then another. Eventually he gets to a point where he is gaining an advantage. With these courts you have to stay in bounds (within the template) to roll each ball.

The courts are ideal for casual, recreation players who want to "step up" a notch without spending big bucks for their own traditional court. Many top players will thumb their noses at this product, but they are not the market for which it was developed. It reminds me of Mike Paccione's Resolver – a tape measure that sits atop a clear acrylic cube that fits over the pallino. The tape swivels 360 degrees (see www.bocceresolver.com). Top players think it is a "toy" – only the most accurate inside measuring device will suffice. But backyard players find it clever, easy, and accurate enough for their level of play.

Many who host Fourth of July cookouts and other family events include bocce as part of the festivities. They can purchase a couple of these courts and offer an organized backyard bocce tournament complete with bracket boards. Now, anyone can be a tournament director!

Companies who host large outings can offer a terrific and cost effective recreational program. Anyone who runs a bocce event can consider running it outdoors to avoid the rental cost of indoor facilities. Heck, now you can run a tournament in a public park just by getting a permit from the recreation director!

Template court in use at a senior center

Vinyl Mesh Enclosed Court

This court is a step up from the white vinyl templates and even features vinyl mesh sideboards. This is a good option for the person who always wanted a court, but couldn't fit it in the budget, or didn't want to sacrifice the back yard to a permanent structure.

Reasonably priced, now anyone can own a bocce court. A bonus is that you can take this one down after the day's games, place it in its carry bag, and store it in the garage until you play again.

Set-up is a little more involved, but not daunting. The written directions are clear and well illustrated, and you need only a cordless drill and a mallet.

The idea is to drill into the ground so that you can drive in some plastic ground anchors every ten feet in a straight line.

Then you insert metal support posts (which you attach to the mesh sideboards) into the ground anchors, taking care to keep that straight line. The process takes 30-45 minutes the first time, but once the ground anchors are in, the set-up time can be cut in half.

{Note: the ground anchors can be eliminated if you think you might want to set the court up in different locations on different occasions. Just drive the support posts directly into the holes that you drill in the ground. Use the ground anchors only if you want a permanent home for your court.}

With all these products, I recommend dropping the wheels on your lawnmower, and

Vinyl mesh court by Backyard Bocce

cutting the grass before play (at least over the section where you'll place the court).

Also, sometimes "standard" size pallinos get obscured by the grass. You may want to use a larger target. A croquet or field hockey ball works nicely. In a pinch, use a baseball or any ball about the size of a baseball.

Chris Pfeiffer's Backyard Bocce, Inc. has done a great service for the bocce playing community. His excellent product line is a boon to Special Olympians, parks and recreations programs, week-end bocce warriors, senior centers, schools and just about anyone else who's ever tried to roll, toss, heave or otherwise direct a bocce ball toward a pallino. Pfeiffer may just revolutionize backyard bocce.

Chianti is the beverage of
choice for court christenings

Chapter 9
Bocce Courts We've Known & Loved ▬

What follows is a bocce court pictorial. Most are outdoor venues, a few are indoors. Starting with my own court in Methuen, Massachusetts, we cover New England, then move south and west, zigzagging and detouring a bit (geography was never my strong suit). The pictorial ends up on the west coast with photographs submitted by David Brewer (Boccebrew.com) and Tom McNutt (Boccemon. com) displaying courts they have built in California and the Pacific Northwest. Enjoy the trip!

Methuen, MA - the author's home – fruit tree lined – 76' by 10' – Har-Tru surface

Barrington, NH - Dante's Pasta and Primo Vino Restaurant – two outdoor, stone dust courts

*Methuen, MA - residence – 64'
by 12' – stone dust*

*Bradford, MA – residence - 45'
by 9' – stone dust (a derringer
among bocce courts)*

*Walpole, MA - Italian American
Club – four lighted 74' by 10'
stone dust/clay mix courts*

*Boston, MA – three outdoor
city-owned stone dust courts
overlooking the Charles River
(Bunker Hill Monument and
Old Ironsides in background)*

*Boston, MA - Steriti Hockey Rink
– two 76' by 10' courts within the
complex (heated & air conditioned)
adjacent to the outdoor courts*

*Springfield, MA - Mt. Carmel
Society – 76' by 10' – stone dust*

Springfield, MA - Elks Lodge – two 76' by 10' lighted, stone dust courts with a topping of "brick dust"

Wilbraham, MA – 76' by 10' lighted court with stone dust surface

Chicopee, MA - Szot Park – three 76' by 10' courts – brick dust surface

Springfield, MA - Forest Park – two 76' by 10' courts – stone dust

Waterbury, CT - Pontelandolfo Club – banquet hall with ten courts on site (four indoors, four outdoors uncovered, two outdoors covered)

Old Lyme, CT – two stone dust courts located on "Bocce Lane"

Old Lyme, CT – "gated communities" with colorful names like Hawk's Nest and Miami Beach – court has stone dust surface

Mount Vernon, NY - Hartley Park - Two indoor courts – 70' by 11' – fine ground stone surface – Guy DeSantis/Mario Taormina photo

Shoreham, NY – residence - 55' by 12' – Har-Tru top dressing – Jim LoScalzo photo

Corona, Queens, NY - William F. Morse Memorial Park - the neighborhood was once home to jazz trumpeter Louis Armstrong - Surrounding area is the fictional setting for the popular TV series "All in the Family"

Queens, NY - Juniper Valley Park – two 73' by 12' courts - Willie Itzkowitz photo

Brooklyn, NY - Carroll Park Gardens – two 75' by 10' courts

Huntington, NY - Heckscher Park - 78' by 13'

Brooklyn, NY - Marine Park Bocce Club – three lighted courts with canopies (summer) - Har-Tru and clay surfaces – Willie & Gloria Itzkowitz photo

Manhattan, NY - Il Vagabondo restaurant – indoor court flanked by dining tables – for safety, they use a washer (not a pallino) as the target

Huntington, NY - Mildam Park – two lighted 78' by 16' courts – home of the Long Island Bocce Club

Valley Stream, NY - A.J. Hendrickson Park - The 42-acre park also has a lake, diving pool, water park, Olympic size swimming pool, basketball hoops, and more

Callicoon, NY - Villa Roma Resort – nestled neatly in the Catskills, all the usual amenities plus indoor and outdoor bocce

Rome, NY - Toccolana Club – six indoor, stone dust courts – hosts the popular World Series of Bocce using Pugliese Pavilion as well

Rome, NY - Jimmy Pugliese Bocce Pavilion – nine covered 60' by 10' courts – site of the popular World Series of Bocce

Easton, PA - Villa Tempo Italiano – Pam Richetta photo

Farrell, PA - American Legion - 2 covered outdoor courts (pictured), 2 indoor - Brian Polantz photo

Mayfield Heights, OH – Mayfield Heights City Park (5 courts) - Brian Polantz photo

Wickliffe, OH - Italian American Club (6 outdoor, 3 covered) - Brian Polantz photo

Canton, OH - Canton Civic Center (Astroturf) - Brian Polantz photo

Baltimore, MD - "Little Italy" – two 80' by 13' lighted courts, stone dust surface

Fearrington Village, NC – two courts dedicated to the memory of local "Mr. Bocce", George "Bus" Detweiler

Chattanooga, TN - Bluff View Arts District – "The Most Scenic Court in the South" - 76' by 10' - brick dust surface (Tennessee River to the right – bed and breakfast to the left).

Griffin, GA – two 76' by 12' courts - rock dust surface – George Danner photo

Hallendale Beach, FL – public park - two 78' by 12' courts – Har-Tru surface - Michael Grasser photo

Punta Gorda, FL — two 60' by 12' courts and one 75' by 12' – note canopies - George Farruggio photo

Pike County Georgia – residence – two 60' by 12' grass courts of T4 Bermuda Turf – Owner cuts grass with a golf green mower and leaves the bordering grass high – Lance Taylor photo

Punta Gorda, FL - Lake Rio Townhouses – 60' by 8' clay court - Jim Smith photo

Punta Cana, Dominican Republic - The Breezes Resort – 42' by 6' - beach sand surface – volo games – tennis ball used as object ball (doesn't get buried in the sand)

Cape Coral, FL – four 70' by 15' clay courts – 45 degree angle boards - Michael Grasser photo

*Sylvan Lake, MI - Four 76'
by 12' limestone and Har-Tru
courts – Michael Grasser photo*

*Pontiac, MI - Vidosh
Landscape Center – 90' by 12'
- crushed limestone surface
– Michael Grasser Photo*

*Sylvan Lake, MI – 60' by 12'
court, later extended to 72' at
landscape architect Michael
Grasser's residence*

*Rochester, MI - 82' by 12.5' -
Michael Grasser photo*

*Rochester, MI – 70' by 18' court
with stone column supported
pergolas – Michael Grasser
photo*

Round Lake, IL - Alpine Country Club – four 84' by 10' synthetic surface courts – private club established in 1886

Round Lake, IL - Alpine Country Club – two 80' by 12' outdoor, covered courts with Har-Tru surface

Centennial Park, Park Ridge, IL – two 80' by 10' courts nestled neatly between Park Ridge's Community Center and Senior Center – Har-Tru surface – heavy plastic sideboards

Collinsville, IL – 70' court on the "high ground" affording a spectacular view of the St. Louis skyline & Gateway Arch – stone dust surface, overhead lighting, covered – Matteo Melucci photo

Highwood, IL - Highwood Bocce Club – two outdoor Har-Tru courts, four indoor 86' by 10' synthetic surface courts

Windsor, Ontario, Canada - Ciociaro Club – five synthetic surface 88' by 11'4" courts - Michael Grasser photo

Woodbridge, Ontario, Canada - Father Ermanno Bulfon Community Center - 5 indoor synthetic surface, 5 outdoor courts - Brian Polantz photo

Tucson, AZ - St. Francis Assisi Church/High School complex - two 70' by 16' courts – compacted fine gravel surface – 45 degree angle boards Michael Grasser photo

Phoenix, AZ – Arizona Italian American Club – four lighted courts - Denise Storace photo

Santa Monica, CA - Christine Emerson Reed Park - Steve Watkins photo

Las Vegas, NV - Jaycee Park – eleven 90' by 12' stone dust courts in the public domain – Michael Grasser photo

Monterey, CA - The Custom
House Plaza in Monterey's
Historic Park – Tom McNutt
photo

Pebble Beach, CA – 60' by 12'
oyster flour court with 18th century
marble statue of centaur holding
an alabaster bust of the Emperor
Nero - David Brewer photo

San Jose, CA - The Villages –
synthetic turf "Sports Courts" by
Grass Tex, Inc. - John Ross photo

Monte Sereno, CA - Shady Oaks
Winery and Bocce Club – 80' by 11'
– oyster shell flour & sand – 500 watt
halogen lights - John Ross photo

Los Gatos, CA - Campo di Bocce
"Eight world-class bocce courts
amid vine covered arbors and
cypress tree shaded seating
areas. " - Tom Ovens photo

Pleasanton, CA – sportscaster
John Madden's residence
– 60' by 10' oyster flour court
– concrete curb, IPE wood
bumpers – David Brewer photo

Martinez, CA - Waterfront Park – 15 city owned courts maintained by the Martinez Bocce Federation – newest court has an asphalt paved base with a thin layer of oyster shell topping – John Ross photo

Hillsborough, CA – refurbished estate built in the 1920's – 60' by 12' oyster flour court – David Brewer photo

South of San Jose, CA – vineyard court – 60' by 12' - oyster flour surface – David Brewer photo

Novato, CA – 60' by 12' oyster flour court - David Brewer photo

Yountville, CA - Villagio Inn and Spa – 60' by 9.5' oyster flour court - wheelchair accessible - Brazilian hardwood benches - David Brewer photo

Cloverdale, CA – 70' by 12' combination bocce and pétanque court – oyster flour surface - David Brewer photo

191

Napa Valley, CA olive ranch – 60' by 12' decomposed granite surface - David Brewer photo

Healdsburg, CA – Heron Hill vacation-rental property — 78' by 12' clay/oyster flour court – John Robbins photo

Healdsburg, CA – 70' by 12' oyster flour court in the Alexander Valley - David Brewer photo

Sonoma County, CA - Landmark Winery – 65' by 10' oyster flour court - David Brewer photo

Angwin, (Napa Valley) CA – an elegant steel swing sits beside 90' by 12' oyster flour court – owner builds caves deep in the mountainsides for the wineries - David Brewer photo

Rutherford, CA (Napa Valley) 60' by 12' oyster flour court - David Brewer photo

Napa Valley, CA - near Francis Ford Coppola's estate – oyster flour surface - "A glass of wine, a bocce ball, and thou." David Brewer photo

Napa Valley – residence – 60' by 12' oyster flour court

Napa Valley, CA – 60' by 12' oyster flour surface - David Brewer photo

Hopland, CA - Brutocao Schoolhouse Plaza - six 90' by 13' crushed oyster shell courts – Sue Brutocao photo

Sacramento, CA - East Portal Park – two 90' by 12' and two smaller courts, all with roof structures for year-round play - oyster flour/sand surface – John Ross photo

San Rafael, CA – "Smallest court I ever built" (42' by 7') – David Brewer

Bellingham, WA - Tom McNutt's 60' by 12' home court bordering a commercial district – McNutt promotes the game to passersby – Tom McNutt photo

Barkley Village, Bellingham, WA – 76' by 12' oyster court – Tom McNutt photo

Chapter 10
Organizing A League/Promoting The Game

To run a bocce league you need players, a venue, and someone with the organizational skills to get the operation on track. To find players, you might start a little publicity campaign, alerting local newspapers, radio, and other media sources. You can post signs at gyms, senior centers, schools, Boys and Girls Clubs, YMCAs or other suitable locations.

Word of mouth is always the "best bang for the buck." Tell everyone you know. Say something like "Hey, we're starting a bocce league next month" while handing them a business card. "If you know anyone who might like to play, please give them my card."

Jim Smith of Methuen, Massachusetts and Punta Gorda, Florida describes the "grass roots" method used to start a recreational bocce program at his Florida condominium complex.

"The idea for bocce came from Tom and Kathy Distel. Kathy left flyers on everyone's condo door to come down by the pool and just have fun playing bocce. It was a way to get everyone out at the same time and socialize. It was so successful that the next year Tom built the court, arranged for the clay, and had it spread and rolled by the time we all got down there after Christmas. Needless to say, with a nice court by Lake Rio, the idea caught on and our numbers grew to the present twenties plus."

Flyers on doors and a couple good people with the drive to get a recreational program off the ground was all it took.

Bocce by Lake Rio

Don't let small numbers dissuade you from starting. Our group started very informally a couple years ago, with a handful of us playing at my home court one morning per week. With each player having his own contact sphere, the word eventually reached many people. In short order we had connected with a neighboring town's bocce gang and started a bocce "circuit", one week playing at my place and the next at theirs.

Soon four members had their own backyard courts. So, we rotated sites, playing at each court once a month. Collecting five bucks per person each game day paid for coffee and pastry, with the surplus going into a "kitty" for other expenses including awards and a season-ending party.

Things went smoothly for a while, until our swelling numbers prompted growing pains.

Dealing With A High Player-To-Court Ratio

Each of our outdoor bocce venues has one court. We like to play with eight players, four per team. We station four players at each end. While one end plays, the other coaches, cajoles, communes, or otherwise kibitzes until it's their turn to roll.

When we grew to twelve players, we created three teams and made one sit out and partake of coffee and pastry while waiting their turn. Sometimes we added another half set of balls, putting six players on a team, each rolling two balls.

When we grew even larger, we played games to six or eight points to shorten the "down time."

One day, we took a different tack. One group played on the court while the other played on the lawn. The winners on the lawn advanced to the court, and the losers on the court moved to the grassy venue.

One group on the court

Other group(s) on the lawn

I had almost forgotten how much I enjoyed playing on the lawn, where "reading the green" comes in handy, and home court advantage really kicks in. I tossed the pallino off my chain link fence knowing full well that if I rolled my bocce ball directly at the closed gate it would carom off, rebound gently, and continue down the slight decline toward the object ball.

Nowadays we set up a Backyard Bocce template court alongside our enclosed court and can keep 16 players active at once. Many of us bocce junkies will play anywhere, on any surface with any equipment and any rule variations. We just want to play!

One final note – a relatively new member of our group has really taken to the sport. He is constructing two bocce courts in his Salem, New Hampshire back yard. Other *Joy of Bocce Weekly* subscribers tell me that they too have built multiple home courts. This can only be an indicator of the game's growth approaching "critical mass".

Getting Started

I've run many sporting events and fundraisers over the last four decades. My experience suggests that you might need to "bite the bullet" and just get the event off the ground, even with a small number of participants. Run a good program, pay attention to detail, and kick it off at the same time every year so that people learn to plan on it. Do a good job and it will grow.

One year, I ran a 3-on-3 basketball tournament for seniors age 50 and over. It was my first time running such an event and, with 14 teams, we had an artistic, if not financial success. Senior hoopers are real junkies – they play year round and travel great distances to compete. With a terrific field house with 6 hoops going at once, excellent referees, and a well-organized schedule, we got an enthusiastic response from the players. The following year, without advertising, teams were calling me to inquire about the tourney. In addition, each year's teams recommend us to other groups that they meet on the tourney circuit. Now, we regularly draw teams from

Massachusetts, New Hampshire, Vermont, Maine, Connecticut, Rhode Island and Delaware. Run a quality program, pay attention to detail, hold it the same time each year. It will grow and flourish.

Get your league started. Leaders will emerge. If you need financing, maybe someone will step forward to organize a fundraiser. Perhaps a member has some political "pull" who can help get courts built in a public park (always go for multiple courts – at least two - with such a campaign). Our bocce posse stands at about forty now, if you count the players who don't play every week, but fill in occasionally. There is a lot of talent in the group – not just bocce talent, but brains, skills, contacts, problem-solving ability – a powerful support group.

Finding A Bocce Venue

You can start your league at the bocce court(s) in a public park (might require a permit to reserve dates and times). You can play at some court owner's house. You could even play in an open field using Backyard Bocce's template courts. Playing on the infield clay or stone dust of a ball field also works nicely. Our senior group plays during the day when kids are in school and the ball fields are available.

Bocce on a ball field

You could advertise Free Bocce Lessons (Meet at Central Park at 5:00 PM) to draw interest. Start out with informal play, then decide if you want to evolve to a league format. If you opt for league play, a Ladder can be used to form balanced teams.

Using A "Ladder" To Form Teams For League Play

A Bocce Ladder is a ranking of players in order of pointing skill. Top level players agree that pointing is more important than hitting, and they will take a good pointer over a good hitter every time. So, initially we need to establish which rung on the "pointing skill ladder" each player will occupy.

Each player rolls 8 balls

We measure the distance from the pallino

After measuring, we move balls out of the way

Every player rolls 8 balls attempting to get as close as possible to the target ball, which we arbitrarily set in the center of the court 16 feet from the end of our 72-foot playing surface. After each rolled ball, we measure its distance from the target, record it, and move that ball out of the way (we want subsequent rolls to have a clear path to the target).

If the target ball is hit by any roll, we return it to its original location and measure the distance from there to the resting place of the rolled ball. For these measurements, a steel tape is best and, since precision is not critical, we measure from the edge of the pallino to the center of the bocce ball (estimate where the center is).

When the eight balls are rolled and their distance from the object recorded, we eliminate the two worst rolls and then total the combined distances of the remaining six.

Using these totals, we rank order the players from first to last in order of pointing skill. The player with the lowest total gets the top rung and the player with the highest ends up on the bottom rung.

This is only the initial positioning. Now, any player may challenge another player who is not more than 4 rungs up the ladder. They play a regular singles bocce game to 12 points.

If the higher seed wins, there is no change to the ladder. If the lower seed wins, s/he takes over that higher rung and the higher seed drops down a rung (pushing some of the others down a rung as well). For example, if #4 challenges and beats #1, #4 earns the top spot on the ladder. One drops to two which pushes the previous #2 to #3 and the previous #3 to #4, (but #5 through the bottom rung are unaffected).

Another simpler option is to just have the winner and loser exchange rungs on the ladder (no one else's position is affected).

Players who join after the initial ladder is set up take the eight ball qualifying test and are inserted into the Ladder in a position relative to the other scores.

Once placed in the Ladder, movement up and refinement of the Ladder is accomplished by challenges.

If you know that certain players ended up lower than they should have, your organizers can initiate challenges for the good of the league.

Set a reasonable period of time for challenges to take place and make a few ground rules such as these from The Long Island Bocce Club (www.libocceclub.com)...

"A member may not challenge the same person more than once in a calendar month."

"A member may accept any number of challenges but is not required to accept more than 4 challenges in any calendar month."

After a suitable period of time for ladder "refinement," it is time to pick teams. Here is an example of setting up 10 evenly matched teams with 40 players (with odd numbers you will have to tweak this to fit your situation).

Pair up the top ranked player with the bottom ranked, second ranked with next to last ranked, etc. on down the ladder.

1-40
2-39
3-38
4-37
5-36
6-35
7-34
8-33
9-32
10-31
11-30
12-29

13-28
14-27
15-26
16-25
17-24
18-23
19-22
20-21

Next match up the first two-player team with the bottom one to make a four-player team.

1-40.....&.....20-21 {These numbers add up to 82}
2-39.....&.....19-22.....= 82
3-38.....&.....18-23.....= 82
4-37.....&.....17-24.....= 82
5-36.....&.....16-25.....= 82
6-35.....&.....15-26.....= 82
7-34.....&.....14-27.....= 82
8-33.....&.....13-28.....= 82
9-32.....&.....12-29.....= 82
10-31....&....11-30.....= 82

Mike Conti of the USBF offers these comments...

"The bocce ladder is a good way to form teams for league play. It is important to balance the teams as much as possible. In the Chicago area we have a committee that classifies the players as A, B, or C.

Each team has at least one of each. Our teams usually consist of three or four players. We also have handicap players, giving them points, such as +1 +2 +3. A team of +1 and +3 = 4, vs. a team +1 +2 = 3, the score would start out as 4 to 3."

Once you have teams formed (your Ladder can be used to create one-, two-, three- or four-person teams), you can create a schedule and start your league. You'll need to decide on playing rules (we highly recommend North American Open Rules - chapter 11 or International Rules - chapter 12).

You may want to evaluate just how organized you want to get. Don't forget - it's supposed to be fun. If you'll collect dues, you'll need a treasurer. You can elect officers or appoint a committee to oversee the schedule and to rule on issues that may come up during the season. For example, our four-player teams were sometimes short-handed on game day (only 3 players showed up).

I did some research on the subject and brought the following information back to the group for a vote…

If you normally station two players at each end of the court, the short-handed team will have two players at one end, but only one at the other end. Many think that if this player rolls four balls, he gains an advantage over his two opponents who roll just two balls each.

Some solutions...

The best answer is to recruit more players. If each team had five players, one absence still leaves you with a full team. When five show up, the captain has to rotate personnel. S/he can tell a player to sit one game or substitute part-way through a game.

Some leagues have a list of "Pool Players." These are players who are willing to fill in occasionally but don't want to be regulars. If you know you are going to be shorthanded, you can contact a pool player ahead of time.

If you decide to allow one player to roll four balls, rotate who will play solo. This way your top player doesn't roll four every game.

Another solution is to "burn" a ball or two for the guy who plays singles. The solo guy can't play four balls, only two or three.

Still another option is to use a "walker." One of the three players rolls two balls with a partner on one end, then walks to the other end to roll two balls with his other partner in the next frame. The walker plays both ends of the court, but only plays two balls at each end like everybody else. If you play three games, you could rotate who will walk each game.

Finally, another thing to consider is that there is a movement gaining momentum to run leagues with three-person teams. You still have four players on your roster, but only 3 are required to field a team. This style of play requires using 12 bocce balls (2 balls for each player) and all six participants walk from end to end. You get a little gentle exercise, and play every frame instead of every other one.

Surprisingly, even though 12 balls are in play, most rounds generally end with just one or two points scored.

Our group opted for the rotating walker. Each of the three teammates acts as the walker in one of our three league games.

Court set-up at Home Run Park

Following is a brief synopsis of our league play that you might use as a model or starting point from which you can adapt for your situation. We play outdoors informally as long as we can. When winter sets in, we move indoors to Home Run Park, one of the old mill buildings in Lawrence, Massachusetts. Home Run Park rents space to baseball and softball players for pitching, batting, and fielding practice. We set 6" by 6" by 8' timbers down on the Astroturf surface, framing off as many as four courts, each measuring about 12' by 72'.

When we move indoors we raise dues to $10 per person with $5 going toward court rental. The rest covers refreshments, awards, and a season-ending banquet. We conclude our indoor season with a small, catered party and we culminate the outdoor season with a bocce clambake and co-ed tournament.

The teams play 3-game matches, once a week for 20 weeks, followed by a couple weeks of play-offs, a break-up/awards party, then move outdoors in April. After each match, we email the results to the local newspapers as well as to all our players. We update the standings on our web site (www.kenwaldiessc.org) which promotes our non-profit group – Ken Waldie Senior Sports Circuit, Inc. Ken was a friend of ours, a naval academy grad, and a victim of 9/11/01. By reporting the scores, we keep his name alive in the newspaper, get a little publicity for sponsors, and increase awareness of bocce.

Promoting The Game

Once your league is running, you'll likely become your area's bocce gurus. You will be in a position to promote the game. Find out who outside your group is playing, and challenge them to a match (even if you have to travel). You'll connect with other like-minded individuals while competing, and perhaps enjoying a cookout or outing as well.

Bocce at the senior center

Consider offering bocce demonstrations. We have done many of these for senior centers, schools, libraries, even pre-schoolers. Janis Cooke Newman, writing in the *NOE Valley Voice* tells us that "Bocce, it turns out, is a perfect game for kids. It's much more about finesse than strength. So not being strong enough to send the ball crashing into the board at the back of the court is a good thing." Ms. Newman also correctly reminds us that "There is no crying in bocce."

Our demonstrations generally include a brief talk on the history of the game, an explanation of how to play, and a quick demonstration of the punto, raffa, and volo shots. Most importantly, we set up games for those in attendance. Get them playing rather than listening to someone tell them about playing. This wonderful game sells itself. We simply need to get the word out and encourage others to try it.

For a demo at our public library we set down two-by-fours on an open, carpeted area, creating temporary courts. The library advertised a free bocce demonstration and parent-child tournament, attracting fourteen teams of middle school aged players and their mom/dads. I gave the usual short talk about the origins of bocce, brief instruction on how to play, then ran a single elimination tournament. The entire program took about 3 hours and it was well received by parents, the children, and the library staff. Two local newspapers showed up to cover the event, each running photos and positive stories.

This good publicity resulted in a request to do a similar event for pre-schoolers. The event was well publicized and about 30 children (mostly 3- to 5-year-olds) showed up at the Bridgewalk Family Resource Center, which offers a variety of free children's programs and parenting services. For the youngest children we used small, brightly colored, plastic balls and made sure there were plenty of adults around for crowd control. We were on the alert for errant tosses and for bocce balls dropped on tiny toes.

Bocce at the library

Bocce with pre-schoolers

We brought the children into the building's old gymnasium, and sat them down for a brief talk about bocce and an even briefer demonstration of how to play. We repeated several times the admonition to "Roll the balls very GENTLY."

Ah, Gently...

Then, before sending the preschoolers off to experience the joy of bocce, we set the tone with some mood music (Frank Cappelli's Bocci Ball). If you are unfamiliar with Cappelli's wonderful melodies, you are in for a treat. Contact him at F.E. Cappelli Publishing Co., 717 North Meadowcroft Ave., Pittsburgh, PA 15216.

We set up 3 sections of carpet on the gym floor and sent the three-, four-, and five-year-olds off to different areas. The older children played bocce games with regulation bocce balls and two-by-fours marking the court boundaries.

When the children tried to pick up two bocce balls at once, they dropped one or the other or both. So, we learned to "Roll the balls GENTLY, and one at a time, please!"

The younger tykes just practiced rolling the small, colorful plastic or water-filled balls. It wasn't certain that they understood the object of the game, but it was infinitely clear that they were having a blast!

Teaching bocce to children in the park

The event lasted just a little over an hour, and before they left, many of the adults asked for more information about the game. So, we not only survived a close encounter with tots armed with bocce balls, we succeeded in spreading the word about the game we love.

We are planning a bocce league for local high school students. Since we can use the bocce balls and scoreboards from our Ken

Waldie Senior Sports Circuit, Inc., we can offer the program very inexpensively (the schools won't have to purchase equipment).

We envision a bocce conference just like in basketball, soccer, or baseball. On game day we'll have several schools competing like a tri- or quad-meet in track. A co-ed sport, there will be four players on a team, with substitutes. Perhaps we will attract the kind of student who wouldn't normally play on an interscholastic team, or maybe we'll get youngsters who can't commit to practice every day, but can play once or twice a week. To stimulate interest, we'll offer demonstrations to the various high school physical education classes.

Introducing bocce at the high school

Of course they love it

Co-ed bocce is always a hit

Once they experience the Joy of Bocce, they're hooked

Promote Your Group With CafePress

If someone in your group can create a bocce logo or art work for your league, you can promote yourselves by putting it on t-shirts, mugs, mouse pads, etc. at no cost, perhaps even making a few bucks for your group.

Probably the best kept secret in fundraising, CafePress is smart, simple to manage, and appropriate for anybody who might want to sell promotional items for their business, hobby, club, or sports team. It's a print-on-demand company. You go to their site (CafePress. com) and set up a "virtual storefront" (easy to do, and no charge). Next, you pick the items from their "virtual supply house" that you want to sell (no charge to you). Now upload your logo/artwork (still no charge). The image will appear on a graphic of the item indicating its cost, and you are prompted to input the sale price you would like to charge (mark it up to whatever price you choose).

That's it. No set-up charge, no minimum quantities to order, no inventory, no risk. You just need to send traffic to that storefront (e.g. "Hey guys, you just gotta check out CafePress.com/joyofbocce"), and encourage people to purchase the items.

When CafePress gets an order (even a single mug, for example), they collect the funds through THEIR merchant account, print the item, ship it to the customer and, after 45 days (allowing for returns), send you the difference between the item cost and your marked-up price.

It's a no-brainer. If sales are generated, you and CafePress make money. If not, no harm – no foul. Anyone who is raising money for any organization, club, sports team, etc. should be doing this. I recommend getting a professional look though. For your bocce

How could you even think of going to work without your Joy of Bocce lunchbox from CafePress?

league, commission a graphic artist to create personalized artwork for you (anybody can get a piece of clip art off the internet – step up and get a customized image that people can identify with your organization).

Shameless Self-promotion

If you set up a CafePress account and list joyofbocce (all one word) in the box for Referral Store ID, my non-profit senior sports group and I will even get a little bonus…thank you very much.

Promote Your Group And Bocce At The Same Time – Run A Tournament

Consider promoting your group and the game by putting on a modest tournament. If you start with a small number of teams, do a good job, and offer the event the same time each year, it will grow. If you do a really good job, it can even be a money-maker for your group.

Tournaments can be Single Elimination, Double Elimination or Round Robin events. The number of teams entered and the number of courts available will determine which style to use. If you have a lot of teams and only a few courts, single elimination is the way to go. With a handful of teams, a round robin is the answer.

Most tournaments are 4-player events, but sometimes we see 2- or 3-player competitions, since organizers feel it is easier for people to round up two or three players per team rather than four. Tournaments can offer Open, Mixed or Co-Ed, or Novice Divisions.

If you want to attract top flight teams, you will have to offer large cash prizes and seek out sponsors to cover that expense. I prefer to run more low-key events that encourage beginners to give bocce a try. For this you have to require a reasonably small entry fee, and provide modest awards like sweatshirts or jackets for the winners and runners-up. For our annual May tournament at Home Run Park, we offer jackets for the winners and sweatshirts for the runners-up, all bearing our Ken Waldie Senior Sports Circuit, Inc. logo.

Single elimination is often used when tournament organizers don't have enough courts available to run a double elimination event. One loss and you are out. Single elimination makes it difficult to draw a lot of teams because people may not want to travel for what might turn out to be just one match. Also, single elimination is a tough sell as far as value for your entry dollar goes.

Double elimination is a more common tourney format. If you lose a game you drop into the losers' bracket, and will then play against others teams who have lost. A second loss will send you packing.

The Amateur Softball Association publishes tournament bracket books that list brackets for single and double elimination events for up to 128 teams (www.usasoftball.org).

Note: When you get to the final four teams, some bocce tourney directors award third place to the team that scores more points in their semi-final loss. In one event, my team lost 12-9 in the semis while the other team lost 12-5. We were awarded third place. Wouldn't it be better for those two teams to play a match for third place? If you have two courts available, it could take place at the same time as the finals.

Round robins are particularly suited to small numbers of entrants. Teams will get more games than with the "two and out" or "two and barbecue" formula. For example, if you had only eight teams in your event, double elimination would guarantee everybody two games and the entire schedule would be 14 or 15 matches depending on whether the "If Necessary" game is played. (One team emerges as the winner of the losers' bracket to challenge the one team that has made it though without a loss. If the losers' bracket team is victorious, that would be the first loss for the winners' bracket team, and this would force the "If Necessary" game).

By changing to the round robin format you could put four teams in each of two brackets and have them play each of the other three teams in their "pool". Now, you can use the results of the round robin to establish seeding (first, second, third, and fourth in each pool). You'll need to have tie-breaker categories ready. Maybe the four teams will finish 3-0, 2-1, 1-2, and 0-3. In this case the seeding is obvious. But if they finish 2-1, 2-1, 1-2, 1-2 you need tie-breakers. You might use 1) record against each other 2) most points scored 3) least points allowed, and 4) coin toss. If time is an issue, you could play shorter games in the seeding round (if you normally play to 12 or 15, play to 8 or 10 just for seeding).

Once seeding is established, one loss and you are eliminated. So, everyone is guaranteed at least 4 games with this format (three in the seeding round). You can have the top seeds "cross over" and play the 4th seed from the other side, and 2 vs. 3 cross over with the losing teams being eliminated. At this point, four teams are eliminated. The remaining four teams play and two are eliminated. The two surviving teams play for the championship. If my math is correct, we've had a total of 19 matches with four teams playing four games, two teams playing five, and two teams competing in six contests.

Another alternative, if you are short of courts or time, would be to have just the top two seeds in each bracket advance to the elimination round. The bottom two seeds on each side are out, but they played three games rather than just the two they may have settled for with the double elimination format.

Your event could include a picnic, family events, or other activities. You could join forces with a charity, and raise money for a worthy cause. Hosting a tournament will raise consciousness about your group and about bocce.

Some Scheduling Tips

For single or double elimination events, draw the teams a couple days in advance, not on the morning of the tournament. Some think it shows fair play to draw the pairings with all participants in attendance. But, it might mean that players travel a great distance, arrive early, and then learn that they don't compete for hours.

Draw the pairings early, then call the team captains to let them know when they will play their first game. If a team has a long drive and is arriving on tourney day, try to schedule their first game in the late morning or afternoon.

It is accepted practice to make allowances so that teams from the same league or geographic area don't face off in the early rounds.

If you know which teams will be the strongest, try to seed them so that they are not all bunched together on the same side of the bracket board. You don't want the final match to be a blow-out with a strong team annihilating a weak one.

Chapter 11
Tournament Play & Rules ████████████

Advancing to the tournament level carries with it a trade-off. You gain the more serious competition that you may desire, but you lose the easy, relaxed atmosphere of play in your backyard, neighborhood park, or the beach. Where there was no pressure, no spectators lining the court, no prize money on the line, there is now a whole different ball game.

With a little research, you can probably find some friendly tournament action, but there is also a good deal of high-level (some might even call it cutthroat) competition. The spectrum runs from those like the low-key "Play for the Prosciutto" tourney in Leominster, Massachusetts to those requiring hundreds of dollars for entry fee and big money prizes for the winners. It's probably a good idea to start at the "prosciutto level" and advance as your skills improve. Many local tournaments feature a relaxed atmosphere with good-natured competition. The players referee their own games, only summoning a tournament official in case of a close measurement or other dispute.

Before you enter a tournament, you should find out certain facts. Call the tournament director, or send for the tourney flier. You'll need to know the tournament format. Is it single elimination (one loss and you're out) or double (two losses)? Is the event for singles, doubles, or four-person teams? If it is for four-player teams, do the players throw two balls each and stay at one end of the court, or do they play one ball each, and play both ends of the alley? Can you bring an additional player to serve as a substitute? What is the winning score in each game...12, 15, 16? On what type surface will the event be played--stone dust, Har-Tru, carpet (some tournaments are run in hotels with temporary courts set up right on top of the wall-to-wall carpeting)? Will the games be indoors or out? What are the dates and rain dates, if any? Is there prize money (tournament purses are mushrooming as bocce gains in popularity)? If so, how many teams finish "in the money?" How many games do you have to win to make it to the "money round?"

Many local tournaments return virtually all of the money collected from entry fees as prize money. They rely on the bar and concession sales to turn a profit. For example, one Massachusetts club hosted a 32-team event, collecting $100 per team for a total of $3200 in entry fees. The winners collected cash prizes on the following scale:
   1st place =$1250
   2nd place =$600
   3rd place =$400
   4th place =$250
   5th place=$150
   6th place=$150
   7th place=$100
   8th place= $100
   Total prize money = $3000 with eight of thirty-two teams (25%) finishing "in the money."

As you can see, you are going to have to adjust to different court surfaces and other situations to make it on the tourney circuit. Once you get the details and decide to enter a tournament, you'll have to line up teammates and send in your application with entry fee. If you have a substitute (a fifth player in a four-member team) the captain must decide who plays in which game(s). Most tournament team captains recommend playing the best players in the early games, using the substitute later. The hope is that the stronger team will keep them out of the losers' bracket as long as possible. When you drop out of the winners' bracket early in a double elimination tourney, it makes it very tough to finish in the money.

Probably the most important question you'll need answered is "What rules will govern the tournament's play?" Generally, the game is played the same way in close geographical areas. It is when you travel to another area that problems are likely to arise. A social club hosting a tournament will use its version of the game as the "official" tournament rules, and there may be any number of "house rules". The winning score, for example, may be 11, 12, 15, 16 or more. At a Connecticut tournament, I chatted with an animated senior citizen visiting from Florida. She was a regular on the bocce courts in her retirement home in the Sunshine State, but refused to play in this event. "I hate this kind of play!" she said. "I don't like the rules," she explained. "The games should go to 11 points, not 12, and tournament games should go to 21."

"Tournament games to 21?" I asked. "That must take forever."

"Oh," she replied without missing a beat. "We have lots of time at the senior center."

In some areas on this continent, international rules are observed. Increasingly, we are seeing tournaments governed by "open rules." These are modified from international rules, eliminating some of the restrictions that complicate and slow the game down. Strict international play calls for marking the positions of balls. The player must call his shot when hitting and, if he misses his target, any scattered balls may be returned to their original positions. Open rules are rapidly gaining popularity. And though one group's idea of open rules might be slightly different from another's, they are very similar.

A Tale Of Open Rules

The bocce generally played in North America is very different from the game played in the rest of the world (which is governed by international rules). International rules are well codified and standardized for two games – 1) punto, raffa, volo and 2) volo. As described in chapter 12, international rules play essentially removes the element of luck from bocce. An errant shot often results in balls being returned to their previous positions. Although groups like the US Bocce Federation vigorously promote the international game, "open rules" are much more widely accepted in the USA.

We open rules players play bank shots off the sidewalls. We roll raffas like in bowling, the ball not lofted over a pre-determined line, but rolling all the way to its target. We don't mark the positions of balls. We don't volo much, and a lot of us like that luck is part of our game.

The problem is that there are many differing sets of open rules. None require marking every ball's position, but all vary in subtle and not-so-subtle ways. Some served a good purpose in their day, but failed to evolve as the game matured on this continent. For bocce to get to the next level, we need to adopt international rules, or accept a standardized set of open rules, or both.

Over a period of two years, I researched and compared rules from the various groups playing this wonderful game. The array of variations is astounding. In some areas they score two points for a "leaner" (ball resting against the pallino). Some mandate that teammates alternate rolls. Some even play that if you score in one frame, you must hand the pallino over to the other team to begin the next. I have a hunch that, if you search hard enough, you might even find players who toss the pallino out last, *after* all the balls have been played.

I've interviewed by phone or in person many of the top players as well as recreational players to get their open rules feedback. In addition, I used my ezine, *The Joy of Bocce Weekly,* as a sounding board, soliciting input from subscribers from all over the continent. Not surprisingly, there was not always agreement among the best players, let alone the backyard, post-barbecue type player. Still, I have listened, asked questions, listened some more, posed follow-up questions, and finally wrote what I call North American Open Rules. I claim no affiliation or allegiance to any group. I'm neutral, like Switzerland. I'm just a guy, a bocce player, a writer, who loves this game and wants to see it grow.

Many of the differences from one group's rules to another are minor, and almost any resolution to the discrepancy would accomplish unification, and be acceptable. A handful of other points are more critical. A little background follows, then the rationale for some of the North American Open Rules.

First off, when you play at your home or local league, play by any rules you like. Hey, the game is supposed to be fun. Whatever makes the game interesting and exciting for you should be the format you embrace. Play the backboard live or dead, use 45 degree angle boards, make the winning score 21, mandate that you must win by two points, put in a "skunk" or "mercy" rule.

There is an undeniable charm to playing the "house rules" at the home team's venue. They'll play by your rules when they visit your court. But, if you run a tournament, we hope you'll consider North American Open Rules.

I agree with world-class player Dr. Angel Cordano who says, "I'd like the rules standardized so that we all play the same way, but I'll play any way at all - I just love to play." Heck, a friend of mine gave me an old U. S. Air Force drawing for a 9' by 60' bocce court complete with 45 degree angle boards in the four corners. I'd love to play on a court like this - it would be great fun. But I wouldn't want to see this promoted nationally - keep billiards on the pool table.

I thought long and hard about whether I was adding more confusion to the bocce rules debate with my North American Open Rules. Would I just be adding another set of rules to bewilder people new to the game? As near as I can figure, I am just about the only person on the continent writing regularly about bocce. My ezine connects bocce players everywhere. I feel a kind of moral imperative to make an attempt at codifying open rules. But let's be clear - I don't want to change the way anyone plays in leagues or backyards. I just want to get the Open Rules standardized for tournament play.

All sports go through a period of evolution and the governing rules do too. When I brag to "young pups" about what a good college baseball player I was, they chide me with "Weren't those the days when it was an out if you caught the ball on the first hop?"

Things change. Sometimes they get better, sometimes worse. I hope that the North American Open Rules represent the next step in the evolution of bocce rules on this continent.

Some Points That Needed Ironing Out
The Rationale

What Court Dimensions Are "Official"?

Any that you want. Build courts to suit your pocketbook and your space limitations. But, bigger courts are preferable - at least 10 feet wide (12 or more is better) by at least 70 feet long (75 to 90 if possible).

How Many Foul Lines?

The international game has one line for pointing, another for hitting, and some open rules mandate multiple lines too. Open rules play doesn't need two lines. Most of us don't use long run-up approaches, so let's keep it simple and use the same line for hitting and pointing (about 10 feet from the backboard should do it).

Can You Step On The Foul Line When Rolling?

Although some international rules allow a player to step on but not completely over the pointing line, open rules players tend to stay completely behind the line. In basketball, if you step on the side- or end-line, you are out of bounds. Cozy right up to the foul line, but stay off of it.

Coin Toss Etiquette

You'd think we could agree on how to execute a simple coin toss. Alas, some rules call for the winner to get the choice of pallino OR color of balls, others indicate that the winner gets BOTH. The color of the balls has almost no bearing on the game, so, to streamline things, let the winner of the toss have the first toss of pallino AND choice of color. In many areas, each team brings its own distinctively colored balls anyway, so the only choice is control of the object ball.

Initial Placement Of Pallino

Some rules mandate that the pallino must come to rest between two lines, 12 inches from the sideboards, beyond this line, not beyond that other one. Let's make it simple. The pallino may come to rest anywhere beyond half court as long as it doesn't strike the endboard. If you aspire to become a top-flight player, be advised that the best pointers tend to keep the pallino out in the middle of the court, away from the sides.

Failure To Place Pallino Properly

There are some rules hanging on circa World War I that give a player three attempts to properly place the object ball. We need to "deep six" that rule. You get one shot at placing the pallino properly. If you fail, the other team gets a chance to place it. If they mess up too, you can keep alternating or have the referee place the pallino (a logical spot would be in the middle of the court's width, halfway between the opposite end's backboard and foul line). In any case, the team that had pallino advantage will always play the first ball.

What Do You Do When You Play The Wrong Color Ball By Mistake?

No harm, no foul. Simply replace the ball with one of the correct color.

What Do You Do When You Play Out Of Turn? (e.g. You Had The Point, Didn't Realize It, And Played Another Ball)

First off, we need to promote what has been termed "preventive officiating." Try to eliminate problems before they arise. Referees, teammates and opponents must stay alert and may call out "Wait a minute...it's not your roll."

Failing that, the opposing team may employ the "Rule of Advantage." That is, they may leave everything as is, or return any moved balls to their approximate previous positions and "kill" or "burn" the thrown ball.

What Do You Do When You Play More Than Your Allotted Number Of Balls? (e.g. You And Your Partner Were Supposed To Roll Two Balls Each, And Instead One Of You Rolled Three)

The rule of advantage applies.

What Happens When A Player Thinks The Frame Is Over And Moves His Team's Balls, The Other Team's Balls, Or The Pallino?

Put the ball(s) back where they were and tell the player to pay attention. Make him stay off the court until the frame is over. Don't let anyone touch any balls until the referee or team captains agree on the score for the frame.

Rather than "burn" balls, award points, or impose some other arbitrary penalty, use preventive officiating. Failing that, put the balls back where they were – we knew which points were in contention. Put them back in contention. Do what good referees in all sports do – try to make sure both teams have an equal chance to win.

When Can You Call For A Measurement?

Any time you want. Do away with the ancient rule that once a team has rolled all its balls, the other team may not request a measurement. Come into the 21st century.

May A Player Walk Down Court To View The Positions Of Balls?

By all means. Come on down and take a peek. But, take care not to disturb the positions of balls, and go right back and take your roll so as not to unduly delay the game. You should want to win because you outplayed your opponent, not because he wasn't sure of what shot to attempt.

Can Players Stay On The Court (Opposite End) When Balls Are Being Played?

No. Players should stay out of the court when another player is rolling. In many areas players only exit the court when another player announces that he is hitting. Stay outside the court. Only problems

225

can arise when players mill around, telling teammates where to play their next ball, giving them a visual target. Often, they mistakenly think the frame is over and start moving balls - Trouble.

Backboard Live Or Dead?

Rules calling for a live backboard gained a foothold years ago and just won't seem to go away. The now defunct International Bocce Association (IBA) disseminated rules and promoted them widely. Initially, these served the sport well. The problem is that the game has evolved and these rules have remained static.

Any ball that hits the backboard should be ruled dead unless it first strikes another ball (or the pallino). This is the way most of the USA is playing now. It makes the game one of skill and finesse. Playing the backboard live is not as skillful as playing it dead.

Some will argue that playing the backboard live does require skill, just a different kind of skill. I'm not buying it. My group has played the backboard live (in preparation for tournaments still using the archaic style). Invariably the pallino gets bumped into a corner with the other team's closest point a couple feet away. Then the opponents have a ball or two left that they could roll behind their backs or between their legs and still score points.

Another illustration: With the red team's last ball, they hit the pallino, knocking it to the right hand corner of the backboard. Red has a ball three feet to the left that is "in" for one point. With the backboard played "live" the green team need only whack their ball against the backboard in between the point ball and the pallino – an easy shot even for a novice. However, if the backboard is played dead, the green team must roll a ball close enough to get the point (less than three feet from the object ball) but not so close that it strikes the backboard (rendering it a dead ball). This takes skill, finesse, touch. This is bocce – banging balls off the back to win a point is more like billiards.

Mark Balls?

Generally, we don't need to mark the positions of balls. But, when a player is hitting, you may want to consider marking the positions of balls that are close to the backboard. If a ball hits another ball on its way to the backboard, it is live and the play stands. If it hits the backboard without first touching another ball, it is dead and removed from the court. The ball may hit no ball, strike the backboard, and then carom into a ball or balls near the endboards. These displaced balls have to be returned to their original locations and therefore those positions may be marked previous to the shot.

Note: Care should be taken in swingboard/backboard construction to deaden the impact as much as possible. This will keep "dead" balls that strike the backboard without first hitting another ball from rebounding and displacing other balls.

Outlaw The Volo?

Please don't – it's such a beautiful shot when skillfully executed. Too bad it is so little used in open rules. Some tourney directors outlaw it for safety, although hard throwing raffa players are more dangerous than volo shooters. Others outlaw volo shooting on short courts (those of the 60' variety) reasoning that the targets are too close, and "easy pickings" for good volo players. Still others curtail its use to prevent damage to court surfaces.

North American Open Rules

First A Couple Suggestions For Running A Tournament...

If you have enough courts, consider reserving one for spectators to give the game a try. Have a charismatic person or two from your group "work the court," coaxing people to step up and attempt a couple rolls. Often there are passers-by or onlookers who, given a little encouragement, would love to give the game a whirl. Make your tournament an opportunity to promote the game.

Suggestion #2 – If we want to compete well with the best teams in the world, we need to promote the international game. As players are exposed to the game, some will aspire to compete internationally. We can help identify those players and point them in the right direction. Set aside 20-30 minutes or so for a demonstration of international play. Contact the USBF to find out who in your area might be available to act as "ambassadors of the international game." If possible, cover his/her expenses for the day.

Perhaps these ambassadors could play an exhibition game, explaining their moves as the contest progresses.

Teams

Teams will be comprised of one to four players.
Singles – each player rolls four balls.
Doubles – each of two teammates rolls two balls.
Triples – add a half set of balls so that twelve balls are in play. Each of the three teammates rolls two balls.
Foursomes – each player rolls one ball and all walk back and forth playing both ends of the court, or two players from each team may be stationed at each end of the court, rolling two balls each.

The Equipment & Court Dimensions

Recommend 107 mm, 920 gram balls and courts at least 10 feet wide and 70 feet long. There shall be three lines marked on the court - one indicating mid court as well as one foul line at each end for pointing and hitting.

Coin Toss To Get Started

The winner of a coin toss will toss the pallino to begin the match, and will choose the color of balls for his/her team.

Tossing the Pallino

A player may toss the pallino any distance, so long as it passes the center line of the court, and does not hit the back wall.

Failure to Properly Place the Pallino

If the pallino toss does not pass the center line, or it strikes the backboard, the opposing team will roll the pallino. The team that originally rolled the pallino will play the first bocce ball of the frame.

If the opposing team also fails to properly place the pallino, the referee shall place the pallino in the center of the court's width, halfway between the backboard and foul line of the opposite end. The team that originally rolled the pallino will play the first bocce ball of the frame.

Foul Lines

Players must stay behind the foul line. It is permissible to cross the foul line only after the ball is released and is on its way to the target.

The Game

The first ball will be rolled by the team who originally tossed the pallino. If that ball hits the backboard, it is dead, removed from the court, and the team must roll again until it establishes the initial point. Otherwise, step aside and do not play again until the opposing team has either rolled one if its bocce balls closer to the pallino, or runs out of balls in the attempt.

Whenever a team gets "in" (closest to the object ball), it steps aside and lets the other team roll. A team rolls until it beats (not ties) the opposing team's best ball. This continues until both teams have played all their bocce balls, after which one point is awarded for each ball that is closer to the pallino than the closest ball of the opposition.

If the initial point is knocked out of the court and the thrown ball also caroms out of the court, it is incumbent on the team with pallino advantage to roll the next ball.

Only one team may score in a frame.

The team who scores in each frame rolls the pallino to begin the next frame. If the frame ends in a tie, no points are awarded, and play resumes from the opposite end of the court with the team that held pallino advantage maintaining it for the next frame.

Players may bank balls off the side walls at any time.

Measurements

Team captains may request measurement of any ball at any time. Players may come to the area of play to observe the positions of balls. They must not unduly delay the game, but quickly return to their foul line to play their next ball. Referees shall enforce this regulation and have the authority to "burn" a delaying team's next ball.

Pallino Out Of Play

Once the pallino is legally in play, it remains in play even if it hits the backboard during the game. The pallino remains in play unless it is knocked out of the court or in front of the mid-court line. If either of these occurs, the frame ends and play resumes from the opposite end.

The team that tossed the pallino for that "dead" frame tosses it again in the next frame.

Backboard Dead

A ball touching the backboard is dead and removed from play unless it first strikes another ball, in which case all balls are valid.

If a rolled ball hits the backboard without first striking (or glancing off) another ball and it then bounces off to strike a stationary ball(s) and/or the pallino, that stationary ball(s) and/or pallino shall be returned to the approximate previous positions. The rolled ball is removed from play.

Court Etiquette

Any time a player is rolling, opposing players must remain quietly outside the court. The players shall not step over the foul line before releasing the pallino or their ball. Substitutions may be made at any time.

Order Of Play Within A Team

Teams may elect to play their balls in any rotation. The rotation may vary from frame to frame; however, no player may deliver more than his/her allotted number of balls per frame. (e.g. in Doubles, each partner will roll two balls).

Wrong Color Delivery

If a player rolls the wrong color ball, simply wait for it to come to rest, then replace it with the correct color.

Playing Out Of Turn

If a player rolls out of turn, the rule of advantage applies. The offended team may accept the results of the roll, or remove the illegal ball from play and return all balls to their approximate positions.

Rolling More Than Your Allotted Number Of Balls

If an individual delivers more than his/her allotted number of balls, the opposing team may accept the result of the illegal roll, or remove the illegal ball and return any scattered balls to their original positions.

Illegal Movement Of Balls Or The Pallino

If a player mistakenly moves a ball or balls, replace it/them to their approximate positions. Keep all players off the court until the frame is over. No one should touch any balls until the referee or team captains agree on the score for the frame. Rather than "burn" balls, award points, or impose some other arbitrary penalty, put things back the way they were, ensuring both teams an equal chance to win.

Shooting Volo

Volo shooting is lofting the ball in the air beyond the center or "in play" line of the court. Tournament directors may prohibit volo play at their discretion.

Winning Score

Games shall go to 12 points (tournament directors may alter this). There shall be no "deuce game" (making it mandatory to win by two points) and no "skunk" rule (first team to 12 points wins – no shut-out at 6-0 or 8-0).

Disputes

Any disputes which cannot be resolved by decent, fair-minded competitors will be ruled on by the tournament director/committee.

Chapter 12
International Play

Bocce is becoming increasingly more popular as a competitive, international sport, with enthusiasts lobbying for Olympic status. The good news is that the International Olympic Committee (I.O.C.) has officially recognized bocce, and this is a major step toward becoming an Olympic medal sport.

There are two sets of rules approved for international play – Punto Raffa Volo and Volo. In Punto Raffa Volo rules, the three different shots are allowed if executed according to the regulations, but under Volo rules only the volo and punto shots may be used. In other words, in the Volo game, if you decide to hit, you must loft, not roll your ball at the target. International Volo players generally use metal balls.

The international court is a large one, 27.5 meters long by 2.5 to 4 meters wide (approximately 90 x 13 feet) for Volo play. For Punto, Raffa, Volo competition, the court may be 24.5 to 27 meters long and 4.0 to 4.5 meters wide (approximately 80 to 88 feet long and 13 to 14.5 feet wide).

International rules are more complicated than open rules, but experienced players maintain that the regulations are not intimidating once you get acclimated. The international game is for purists, eliminating the element of luck. For example, you try to knock your opponents' point away with a volo, and your shot is off target, hitting another ball instead. This results, by chance, in your team winning the point. Purists reason, why should you gain an advantage with a poor shot? By international rules, if your ball didn't land within a specified distance of its target, it may be removed from play, and all balls disrupted by the volo attempt returned to their original positions.

As in the rules for other major sports, there is a *rule of advantage* option. Simply stated, if your opponent makes an illegal play that benefits your team, you have the option of accepting the result of the play.

In international games, referees mark the positions of live balls and, not unlike billiards, players call their shots. If a player attempts a knockaway shot and misses, displacing other balls in the process, those displaced balls may be returned to their original positions (which were previously marked on the court surface). Referees use a specialized measuring device/ marking tool to spot the positions of balls and to trace arcs on the court surface. These arcs serve as boundaries for legal landing points for volo shots. As you

International measure - section in center slides left & right along shaft

might guess, these games take longer than those played with Open Rules. Tournament directors sometimes set arbitrary limits, such as declaring the game over at 15 points or 90 minutes, whichever comes first.

Proponents of the international game argue that a game to 12 points will not last any longer than an open rules game where many players delay the action by making frequent trips to mid-court to confer with teammates. International referees oversee a time limit between shots and forbid such delaying tactics.

Still, critics of the international style claim that it is too complicated and makes the game too long. The American people will prefer a quick and simple game, they maintain. And if a pro bocce tour ever comes to fruition, television coverage will demand a fast-paced, action-packed game. Others counter that, when bocce enters the Olympic arena, international rules will prevail. Americans should learn the game on the large court, and with the rules that will allow them to pursue the dream of one day representing the United States in international competition. Donna Allen of the USBF, strongly recommends that any schools constructing courts build them to international specifications. "Build a backyard court to whatever dimensions fit your property and make you happy," she advises. "But build international-sized courts in the schools, and give our young people the opportunity to represent their country."

"You have to witness international rules compared to the open rules," says Dr. Angel Cordano, a retired pediatric researcher and bocce junkie who travels the world to compete. "It's the difference between chess and checkers." Cordano refers to international play as "the real game, where Mr. Luck is a third-rate citizen."

A Summary of the
PUNTO RAFFA VOLO REGULATIONS
of the Confederation Boccistica Internationale

Reprinted with permission of the United States Bocce Federation
Mike Conti, President

{This unofficial summary of the C.B.I. regulations was prepared by the United States Bocce Federation. It is intended only to be an abbreviated guide to the most frequently used rules. Any questions must be resolved by using the complete text of the official C.B.I. regulations}

I. THE COURT.

Metric Conversion:

4 m = 13' - 1-1/2"

7 m = 22' – 11-1/2"

9 m = 29' – 6-1/4"

24.5 m = 80' – 4-3/8"

27 m = 88' – 6-3/4"

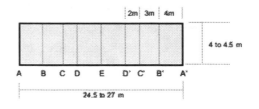

Lines A and A' = coincide with the end of the court and indicate the limit from which players can start their throw.

Lines B and B' = indicate the maximum limit allowed to the players to throw the pallino, the point shot, and the raffa shot. The opposite lines B' and B indicate the maximum distance the pallino can be thrown.

Lines C and C' = indicate the maximum distance allowed to the players for a volo shot.

Lines D and D' = indicate minimum distance a raffa shot must first touch the court, and the limit to which players can go when making a point shot, unless the player is out of balls.

Line E = (mid court) indicates the minimum distance that the pallino must be thrown, and the limit to which players can go when making a raffa or volo shot.

II. THE MATCH

Each match consists of three games. First you play three against three with each player having two balls. Next, you play a singles game, with each player having four balls. Finally you play a doubles game, and again each player has two balls. A substitution can be made at any time after a ball has been played. However, there are no substitutions in the singles game, and no player can participate in more than two of the three games in the match. Championship games normally go to 15 points, but preliminary rounds can go to 12 or 13 points at the discretion of the tournament committee. Only one team scores in a frame. One point is given for each ball that is closer to the pallino than the closest ball of the opposing team. The location of the pallino and balls of each team must be distinctively marked on the court by the referee.

III. STARTING THE MATCH

A. The Beginning:

Each game of a match begins with the referee placing the pallino in the center of the court between the B & E lines. The winners of the coin toss may play the first ball, or choose the end from which to begin. If the choice is made to play the first ball, the opposing team can choose the end from which to begin. If the first ball played is invalid, the same team must play again until they have played a valid ball.

B. The Pallino:

During the game the pallino is tossed by the winner of the previous round. If the toss is invalid, the opposing team tosses the pallino. If that toss is also invalid, the pallino is placed in the center of the court between the B & E lines by the referee. In any event, the first ball is played by the team that first tossed the pallino. You should always wait for the assent of the referee before tossing the pallino. The pallino toss is valid if it passes (not touches) the E line, stops before (does not pass) the B line, and does not touch or stop within 13 cm of the sideboard. If after a valid play, the pallino moves in front of or on the E line, or the pallino leaves the court, the play stops and is resumed from the original starting point.

IV. PUNTO, RAFFA, VOLO

A. Punto:

1. When pointing, a player's foot may be on but not over the B line. The roll is invalid if the player passes the D line after releasing the ball, unless the player is out of balls.

2. A ball that hits the sidewall without first hitting another object is invalid. The opposing team can apply the Rule Of Advantage and leave the rolled ball in its final position or remove the ball from the court.

3. If there is a tie for point, the team last playing plays again until the tie is broken.

4. If the rolled ball hits another ball or pallino (object) and the struck object travels more than 70 cm, the opposing team can elect to return the struck object to its original position and remove the rolled ball from the court, or leave all balls in their final position (Rule of Advantage). If several balls are struck and no single object travels more than 70 cm, everything is valid. If the rolled ball hits an object causing the object to hit the side or back wall, everything is valid unless the struck object traveled more than 70 cm (measured from original mark to the point of impact on the wall and then to the final position of the struck object.

5. If a struck object subsequently hits another object (chain sequence) and the distance from first point of impact to the final position of the last object is greater than 70 cm, the opposing team can apply the Rule of Advantage and leave all objects in their final position or return all objects to their original position and remove the rolled ball from the court.

6. A rolled ball that hits one or more objects which do not travel more than 70 cm, but the rolled ball travels more than 70 cm from the first point of impact, is an invalid throw. The opposing team can apply the Rule of Advantage and leave all objects in their final position or return the struck object or objects to their original positions. In either case, the rolled ball remains in play and is not removed from the court.

B. Raffa:

1. The raffa shot must be made from the B line, and the ball must first touch the court after the D line. If the mark made on the court by the impact of the thrown ball touches or "breaks" the D line, the shot is invalid.

2. Before taking a raffa shot, you must inform the referee that you intend to raffa and which object is your target.

3. If the raffa shot is invalid, the opposing team may apply the Rule of Advantage and leave all objects, including the thrown ball, in their final positions, or return all objects to their original positions and remove the thrown ball from the court.

4. The raffa shot must be released before the player's foot goes over the B line (on the line is valid). The raffa shot is invalid if the player passes the E line after releasing the ball.

5. To be valid, the raffa shot must first hit the declared target or any object within 13 cm (about 5 inches) of the target (bersaglio).

6. You may raffa any ball including your own, provided that the declared ball is located past the D line. The pallino is always a valid raffa target no matter where it is on the court. The raffa shot can not be used on any ball located between the E and D lines unless the target ball is within 13 cm of the pallino (bersaglio).

C. Volo:

1. Before taking a volo shot, you must inform the referee that you intend to volo, which object is your target, and wait for the referee to mark a 40 cm arc in front of the declared target. The referee must also make a 40 cm arc in front of each ball located within 13 cm of the declared target.

2. The volo shot is valid if it strikes any object within 13 cm of the declared target, and the shot hits the court within 40 cm of the struck ball. If the mark made on the court by the impact of the thrown ball touches or "breaks" the arc, the shot is invalid.

3. If the volo shot is invalid, the opposing team can apply the Rule of Advantage and leave all objects including the thrown ball in their final positions, or return all objects to their original positions and remove the thrown ball from the court.

4. The volo shot must be released before the player's foot goes over the C line (on the line is valid). The volo shot is invalid if the player passes the E line after releasing the ball.

5. You may volo any ball including your own or the pallino.

EXAMPLES OF PUNTO RAFFA VOLO REGULATIONS

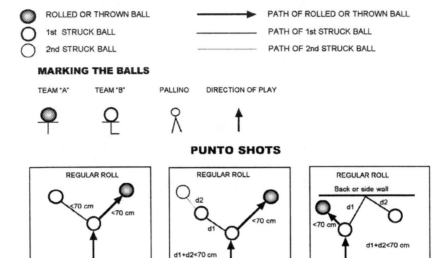

ROLLED OR THROWN BALL   PATH OF ROLLED OR THROWN BALL

1st STRUCK BALL   PATH OF 1st STRUCK BALL

2nd STRUCK BALL   PATH OF 2nd STRUCK BALL

MARKING THE BALLS

TEAM "A"   TEAM "B"   PALLINO   DIRECTION OF PLAY

PUNTO SHOTS

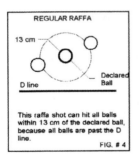

REGULAR ROLL

<70 cm   <70 cm

When the rolled ball moves an object less than 70 cm, everything is valid, provided that the rolled ball also travels less than 70 cm.

FIG. # 1

REGULAR ROLL

d2   d1   <70 cm

d1+d2<70 cm

None of the struck balls traveled more than 70 cm and the rolled ball traveled less than 70 cm after impact.

FIG. # 2

REGULAR ROLL

Back or side wall

d1   d2   <70 cm

d1+d2<70 cm

Total distance from hit to back or side wall to final position of struck ball is less than 70 cm. Rolled ball traveled less than 70 cm.

FIG. # 3

RAFFA SHOTS   VOLO SHOT

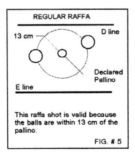

REGULAR RAFFA

13 cm

D line   Declared Ball

This raffa shot can hit all balls within 13 cm of the declared ball, because all balls are past the D line.

FIG. # 4

REGULAR RAFFA

13 cm   D line

Declared Pallino

E line

This raffa shot is valid because the balls are within 13 cm of the pallino.

FIG. # 5

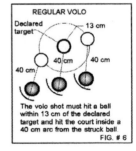

REGULAR VOLO

Declared target   13 cm

40 cm   40 cm

40 cm

The volo shot must hit a ball within 13 cm of the declared target and hit the court inside a 40 cm arc from the struck ball.

FIG. # 6

A Punto Raffa Volo Rules Recap

As you can see, the international game is very different from the bocce most of us "hackers" know. Highly structured and a bit complicated until you get the hang of it, I think I have the hang of it, and here present my thoughts in the clearest English I can muster… {special thanks to Mike & Lois Conti, Joe Giolli, Ron Jacobs, Mike Grasser, Mike Lapcevich, John Ross, and Danny Passaglia who answered my never-ending questions}.

A true international match consists of a singles, a doubles, and a triples competition. You must win two of these three games to win the match. Winners of matches advance to play other winners until an eventual champion is determined. Sometimes tie-breakers (record against each other, most points scored, fewest points allowed) are needed to crown a victor.

The international court has a lot of lines. One is four meters from the end. This line is for pointing and raffa hitting. Raffa is the fast rolling style of hitting as opposed to the aerial volo shot.

For pointing you can have your foot on, but not completely over, the line. Some players walk forward after releasing the ball to ensure accurate momentum in the proper direction. Raffa players use a walk or run-up delivery. They also follow through by continuing forward after releasing the ball. In both pointing and raffa hitting, the ball must be out of the player's hand before s/he crosses the line.

A second line is another three meters forward. This is the volo line. Players use a longer run-up approach when they volo, hence the additional distance.

Two meters farther ahead is a third line which is the minimum distance a raffa shot must travel before it first strikes the ground. In other words, your raffa attempt must be lofted over this third line, then roll the rest of the way to its target.

Finally, there is a mid-court line beyond which the first toss of pallino must come to rest to begin each frame.

Let's call the endboard point A, and these previously described lines B, C, D, and E respectively. Down at the other end of the court you have another endline A or A' if you like, as well as lines B, C, and D.

International rule makers don't want the pallino too close to the sideboards or too near the ends. Thus, the initial toss of pallino each frame may not come to rest less than 13 cm from either side board or beyond the B line at the court's opposite end.

The game is called Punto Raffa Volo because you can employ all three shots. But there are restrictions. The international rules committee decided that hitting an opponent's ball that is near mid-court is relatively easy for accomplished players, and declared the space between line E and the other end's line D to be the volo zone. If you want to hit a ball that rests in that area, you must do so via volo.

You may raffa anywhere beyond that volo zone (the greater the distance the tougher the shot) and you may volo anywhere on the court (volo generally is more difficult than raffa). Also, you may raffa the pallino no matter where it lies on the court {the international pallino is tiny – from the stands it looks like a table tennis ball}.

*Note the heavy duty swing
boards and tiny pallino used
for international play.*

Players who want to hit a ball away must call their shots. The referee uses chalk to mark the positions of all balls and the pallino. You must call which ball you will hit and whether you will do so via raffa or volo. If you declare that you will raffa one ball and hit another by mistake, the Rule of Advantage applies. That is, your opponent can decide to let the play stand, or put the displaced balls back where

*The referee marks with chalk
the position of all balls.*

they were and remove the raffa attempt from play. Exception - if the ball you hit was within 13 cm of the declared target, all is forgiven. This qualified as a *bersaglio*, and is therefore a legal hit.

If you call a volo shot, the referee traces an arc 40 cm in front of the ball you intend to hit. Your ball must land within that arc for it to be a valid hit. If not, the Rule of Advantage applies and the other

*The referee scribes an arc 40
cm in front of the target ball
for an attempted volo.*

team may either leave the play as is, or "burn" the ball and replace all the displaced balls to their previously marked positions.

When I first viewed international play, the trajectory for most volo attempts was lower than I anticipated. Players tell me that the lower shot doesn't bounce as high, which means you can be a tad short and still hit your target. Also, the higher the toss the greater the distance the ball travels. A greater distance makes for a greater degree of difficulty.

Some Rules And Points Of Emphasis...

If you hit the backboard without first hitting another ball, your ball is dead and removed from the court. When the pallino is close to the end line where it is difficult to lag without hitting the back wall, a player often rolls his ball short (just past the volo zone) so that he or his teammate can raffa it to the end with the next shot. For good hitters, this is easier than outlagging a point near the end where you have to worry about striking the back wall and "burning" your ball.

You may not hit the sideboard (Rule of Advantage applies).

All balls must be in the rack unless it is your turn, and you are about to roll. The referee and opponents, by checking the rack, can easily see how many balls are still to be played.

After you have played all your bocce balls, you are to move to the mid court area {this lets everyone know that you have no rolls left this frame}.

Players stay on the court while teammates or opponents play their shots. Although they might inadvertently interfere with play, players stand to the side and closer to the end from where the shot is originating. Displaced balls tend to move away from

After players have rolled their allotted balls, they move down court and take a position so that any displaced balls will not strike them.

them, not toward them. In addition, all balls are marked and can easily be returned to their proper positions.

You must ask the referee's permission to come down court to view the positions of previously played balls. Fail to do so and you forfeit one ball.

Players may get referee's permission to come down court to examine the positions of previously played balls.

The referee uses a 70 cm tool for measuring and marking. If the referee holds this tool straight up (perpendicular to the ground) he's indicating that you took the point with your last roll. Holding it in a horizontal plane means the other team is still in.

The tool has a sliding section that can be used to measure. Players can ask the referee how far away a ball is and s/he can illustrate the distance by holding the tool up to the players' view.

Some Stickier Points

Notice that international rules allow you to step on but not completely over the pointing line.

Displacing another ball even when you are pointing can create a Rule of Advantage situation. If your ball taps another ball causing it to move a distance greater than the length of the tool (70 cm) the rule applies (with fast-playing surfaces, it doesn't take much of a hit to move a ball 70 cm).

Moreover, if your ball moved the pallino just a short distance and caromed off to hit another ball, and that ball moved more than 70 cm, the other team has the option of putting the pallino back to its original position, but the displaced ball stays put.

Bersaglio – when a ball is within 13 cm of the pallino or when two balls are within 13 cm of each other, a bersaglio exists. This means you can call your shot and hit either of the two balls to make a legal hit. Also, you can raffa when there is bersaglio no matter where the balls are. Because of this, sometimes a pointer doesn't want to get too close to the object ball. For example, if the ball was 14 cm away and in the volo zone the opponent would have to volo. But if it were 13 cm or closer they could raffa.

Bocce facility in Campione, Switzerland with seating for 2000 people. Photo courtesy of United States Bocce Federation

Settignano Bocce Club, Atina, Italy

Caccialanza Bocce Club, Milano, Italy

*2003 World Championships
held at Maplensa Athletic
Facility - Chiasso, Switzerland
- Michael Grasser photos*

*World renowned player
Emiliano Benedetti*

*Dismantling court to make
room for more bleachers
for the finals. Complex
used for basketball, hockey,
volleyball, soccer, etc.*

*View of Lake Lugano from
Hotel Serpiano where the
USA team was housed*

*Acrylic barriers
at the ends of courts*

VOLO REGULATIONS
of the Federation International de Boules

(This unofficial summary of the F.I.B. regulations was prepared by the United States Bocce Federation. It is intended only to be an abbreviated guide to the most frequently used rules. Any questions must be resolved by using the complete text of the official F.I.B. regulations)

The aim of the game is to place one's ball as close as possible to a target ball that is called the jack. The opponent, in turn, attempts to place their balls closer to the jack or move the balls that prevent them from doing so. The winning team is the one which first reaches the specified score within the maximum time allowed or has the higher score at the end of regular time.

I. THE COURT

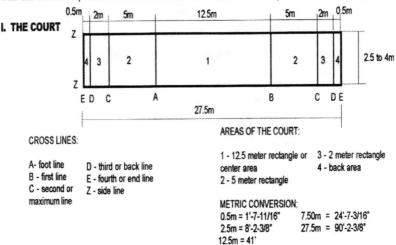

CROSS LINES:

A- foot line
B - first line
C - second or maximum line
D - third or back line
E - fourth or end line
Z - side line

AREAS OF THE COURT:

1 - 12.5 meter rectangle or center area
2 - 5 meter rectangle
3 - 2 meter rectangle
4 - back area

METRIC CONVERSION:
0.5m = 1'-7-11/16"
2.5m = 8'-2-3/8"
12.5m = 41'
7.50m = 24'-7-3/16"
27.5m = 90'-2-3/8"

250

II. STARTING THE GAME.

The right to toss the jack in the first end (frame) is decided by a coin flip. Subsequently, the team winning an end tosses the jack. Any member of a team may toss the jack without being obliged to play the first ball. The delivery is valid when the jack comes to rest in the 5m rectangle opposite the end from which it was tossed (between the B and C lines). If a team fails to validly toss the jack after two attempts, the opposing team places the jack where it wishes within the square, as long as it is at least 50 cm from all boundary lines of the square.

In any event, the team which tosses the jack must play the first ball. The opposing team plays until they take the point or play all their balls. If the first ball goes out of play or is annulled, the opponent must play. If their ball also goes out of play, the first team plays again, and so on. If no balls are left on the court after a valid roll or throw, the opposing team must play. If this last ball played goes out of play or is annulled, the other team must play again, and so on. When each team has a ball equidistant from the jack, the team that played last plays again. If the tie is not broken, the other team plays and so forth until the tie is broken. If a player plays someone else's ball by mistake, simply replace it with the correct ball.

An object is out of play if its central circumference passes beyond the outer limit of the line (side line Z, or third line D) or touches the side wall. The jack is also out of play if its central circumference does not reach past the first or B line.

III. ROLLING THE BALL

Every ball must be played within a maximum time of 45 seconds which starts from the time when:
    a) the jack is correctly placed in the court;

b) it has been decided which team shall play;

c) the referee has made his decision;

d) the required replacements of displaced objects have been made.

In case of infringement the referee will at once annul the ball and it must not be played. If it is played it has no effect.

A rolled delivery is regular when the ball:

a) does not go out of play;

b) reaches to at least 2 meters from the first line;

c) does not move any object more than 50 cm from its original position;

These three conditions must all be satisfied at the same time.

IV. THE THROW

The player who wishes to throw (or shoot) must clearly designate the object which is the intended target. There can only be one target, and it may not be a ball of the player's own team. A mark will be drawn by the opponents 50 centimeters in front of the designated object. This mark must be curved and from 15 to 20 cm in length. Every mark which is not challenged before the throw is valid for checking the point of landing. When the designated object is surrounded by other objects, the curved mark must extend in the necessary direction. Additional throw marks must be made in front of each object situated less than 50 cm from the designated object, providing that such marks are within a circle concentric to the external perimeter of the object and placed 50 cm away from the object.

A throw is regular when all three of the following conditions are met:

a) the point of landing is not more than 50 cm from the designated object;

b) the point of landing is not more than 50 cm from the object first struck;

c) the object first struck is not more than 50 cm from the designated object (measured from the maximum diameter of the objects in question);

The outer edge of the throw mark must not be modified or erased by the impression left on the court by the thrown ball at its point of landing.

A throw is also regular when a ball strikes directly, i.e. without having first touched the court, an object positioned at not more than 50 cm from the designated object. However, in the case of a regular throw with a non-designated jack, the jack is compulsorily restored to its original position.

V. THROW AT THE JACK

If, during an end, the two teams still have one or more balls to play, the jack may be designated once by each team. (This does not apply when balls still to be played belong to only one team.) If the declared jack is struck by a regular throw and there are still unplayed balls belonging to both teams, the end is nullified and will be played again in the same direction. In this case the jack is thrown by the team that had originally thrown it. A non-designated jack hit by a regular or irregular delivery is always replaced to its original position.

If only one team has balls remaining and a declared jack is struck after a regular throw, the throwing team receives one point for each ball that has not yet been played. There is no restriction on the number of throws which may be made on the jack in this situation, except that the last remaining ball may not be thrown at the jack.

VI. ADVANTAGE RULE

All irregular deliveries are left to the discretion of the opposing team. It may:
a) accept the whole new situation thus created, and can either accept or annul the irregular ball;
b) demand the general replacement of all objects to their original positions with the compulsory annulment of the irregular ball.

VII. POSITION OF PLAYERS

In all cases, when not rolling or throwing the ball, all players must stand to the side of the square where the jack is positioned, one team on each side of the court, beyond the first line. At the moment of the throw, the players must stand still and not stare at or do anything to distract the thrower. If space permits all players will keep off the court, as near as possible and along the side line.

EXAMPLES OF THE REGULATIONS
See diagrams

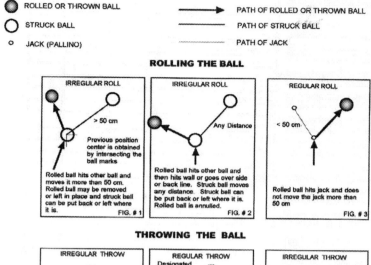

EXAMPLES OF VOLO REGULATIONS

🔴 ROLLED OR THROWN BALL   ➡ PATH OF ROLLED OR THROWN BALL

⚪ STRUCK BALL   —— PATH OF STRUCK BALL

○ JACK (PALLINO)   ········ PATH OF JACK

ROLLING THE BALL

IRREGULAR ROLL

> 50 cm

Previous position center is obtained by intersecting the ball marks

Rolled ball hits other ball and moves it more than 50 cm. Rolled ball may be removed or left in place and struck ball can be put back or left where it is. FIG. # 1

IRREGULAR ROLL

Any Distance

Rolled ball hits other ball and then hits wall or goes over side or back line. Struck ball moves any distance. Struck ball can be put back or left where it is. Rolled ball is annulled. FIG. # 2

REGULAR ROLL

< 50 cm

Rolled ball hits jack and does not move the jack more than 50 cm FIG. # 3

THROWING THE BALL

IRREGULAR THROW

50 cm

Thrown ball is irregular because its point of impact broke the 50 cm arc. Opponents may apply the rule of advantage FIG. # 4

REGULAR THROW

Designated ball

50 cm 50 cm
50 cm

All balls within 50 cm of designated target are marked with an arc. To be valid, thrown ball must hit within 50 cm of designated target and within 50 cm of ball actually struck. FIG. # 5

IRREGULAR THROW

Designated ball

Struck ball

50 cm

Point of landing

This shot is invalid because the point of landing is more than 50 cm from the designated ball. FIG. # 6

A Volo Rules Recap

I first witnessed Volo play at the US Bocce Championships held at the Highwood Bocce Courts, Highwood, Illinois. The Highwood courts have a fast-playing synthetic surface that might have been damaged by volo shooting (volo entails tossing metal bocce balls into the air in an attempt to displace an opponent's ball or the pallino). If you want to hit a ball, you must first call your shot, then strike it with a volo attempt – no raffa, or fast rolling hitting is allowed.

The tournament directors put down a temporary carpet to protect the synthetic surface. This inevitably produced a few surface bubbles as well as some complaints from participants, but the event was extremely well-run and the carpet necessary for the venue to safely host this event.

A little sand sprinkled over the balls makes it easier to mark their positions on the carpet.

Since the ball and pallino are marked. If necessary, the referee can return displaced balls to their original positions.

Each end of the court is marked with three white lines. From the back wall these measured .5 meter, 2.5 meters, and 7.5 meters. Any ball that passes the ½ meter mark is "dead" no matter how it gets there. To begin a frame, the pallino must come to rest between the 2.5 and the 7.5 meter lines. Also, the 7.5 meter mark is the foul line for both pointing and hitting.

Balls that pass the last white line (1/2 meter from back wall) are dead no matter how they got there.

It is a little easier to "zone in" for pointing in this game since the object ball is always within a couple meters of the same place. In Open Rules, for example, you could place the pallino anywhere from mid court to the back wall – a big variation if you are playing on a long court.

When pointing, your foot must be completely behind foul line (as opposed to the other international game - Punto Raffa Volo - where your foot may be on the line).

The side walls are dead (court surface is canted at both sides to minimize chances of balls hitting sides). European volo courts often have no sideboards.

If the pallino touches the boards the frame is over.

Every hit must be a Volo, whereas in (Punto Raffa Volo) a fast-rolling hit (raffa) can be employed.

When you call a shot, the referee scribes a 50 cm arc in front of the target ball. Your ball must land within this arc to be a valid hit, otherwise the Rule of Advantage applies. A volo that lands on the line delimiting the traced arc is invalid. Restrictions are the same as in Punto Raffa Volo play except you cannot call your own ball. Also, unless you designate the pallino as the target, a displaced pallino is always returned to its previous position whether or not the volo shot was valid.

To knock a ball away, you must first call your shot, then loft the ball to within at least 50 cm of the target.

No matter how the balls are scattered by the called shot, we can tell by the arcs if the ball fulfilled the necessary requirements. The referee can check the mark left by the ball when it struck the court surface. If the ball struck a ball on the fly, the referee can view the marked position of the ball that was struck.

Rule of Advantage, as in Punto Raffa Volo play, means that the offended team can take the result of the play or "burn" the illegally tossed ball and replace all displaced balls to their previous positions.

If a rolled ball results in the displacement of any object a distance equal to or greater than 50 cm, the opposing team may "burn" the ball and return the moved balls to their previous positions.

Note: the positions of all balls are marked.

After rolling or shooting you must go to the other end so as not to interfere with the next player's roll.

Some Final Volo Points

The metal volo balls (brass or other alloy) are a tad smaller than the traditional 107 mm plastic composition balls and some contain a special rubber material in the core that absorbs bounce. So, you can hit just in front of the target and, instead of bouncing over, your shot is likely to strike its intended target.

Brass balls are a tad smaller than the traditional ones and are similar in color, but have markings to differentiate one player's from another's.

When pointing, you don't have to worry so much about displacing balls 50 cm, as their mass and composition is such that they don't roll too far after being struck, even on fast surfaces.

Sometimes it is difficult to distinguish one team's bocce balls from another's (colors are similar), but distin_ctive lines etched on the balls' surface make for easy identification on closer inspection.

In international play we mark the positions of all balls and the pallino.

Variation in the size and weight of balls is allowed within certain parameters.

Games are long – matches may go to a set number of points (generally 13 or 15) or to a time limit (1 ¼ hours to 1 ½ hours) or to whichever comes first.

*Team USA 2003 - Nice,
France World Championship*

Special Events

(Precision Shooting - Rapid Progressive Shooting – Combination)

Some international competitions feature "shoot-outs" reminiscent of the NBA three-point shoot-out. Officials place balls in different positions and at different distances from the shooter (using a specialized mat which has eleven different positions at which a target ball or pallino is placed). The balls are side-by-side, one in front of another, even behind the pallino. One to five points are awarded for successful hits based on the degree of difficulty for the particular shot. For this Precision Shooting, players generally get two attempts at each target, proceeding in a pre-determined sequence, and keep a cumulative score. Contestants can rack up a maximum of 37 points.

The Rapid Progressive Volo Shooting is an event where target balls are placed on pre-positioned locations on mats located at each end of the court. The contestant runs to the 7.5 meter line and lofts his shot at the target, and then runs to the other end, picks up a ball from a stand, and repeats the process back in the opposite direction.

There are six target spots on each mat located .8 meter apart. After each hit, the target ball is placed in the next position (.8 meter farther away). After the last target is struck, the targets are moved progressively forward and so on. The exciting event lasts 5 minutes.

Contestants in this event are physically fit and train like 1500 meter track athletes. John Ross of the USBF informs us that the world record is 52 hits in 54 attempts, adding… "Imagine a 1500 meter runner throwing a 2-1/2 lb. ball every 30 meters along the way and hitting a 4 inch target 40 to 60 feet away with 98 to 100% accuracy!"

To recap, for this event a mat is used, upon which are placed target balls. As a player makes a good hit, the target is progressively moved farther back from one to six designated spots on the mat. When you hit the first target, a "spotter" places the target ball in the second position on the mat. {There are six positions on each mat, and a mat at each end of the court. You have five minutes to run back and forth, hitting as many targets as you can within the time limit. It is ironic that, to the uninformed, bocce conjures up images of old, out-of-shape wine drinking, cigar smokers, while this demanding event rivals any cardiovascular endeavor one can imagine.}

Players use a palm down release intended to hit the target on the fly.

After the shot is released, the player runs to the other end of the court.

There he takes another ball off the stand and proceeds to shoot at the target at the opposite end. Note spotter.

The target (in spot #1) stays until it is successfully struck.

There are six spots on the mat.

A hit prompts the spotter to move the target back one notch.

The player tries for as many hits as possible in five minutes.

The final target.

The Combination Event

The combination event consists of eight frames. One contestant lags the pallino. Once the object ball comes to rest, a 70 cm radius circle is drawn around it.

One contestant then lags into the circle using the pallino as a target. If the ball enters and stays in the circle, one point is earned by the lagger. The other contestant then shoots, attempting to knock the ball out of the circle. One point is awarded for each hit. Each player has four balls. At the completion of the first frame, they resume from the opposite end except that the contestants reverse roles.

There are always four shots in every frame. A "par" score would be 32, but two points can be earned if the lag comes within .5 cm of the pallino or touches the pallino.

Also, if the shooter's ball stays within the circle after a successful hit, 2 points are awarded. Even if you don't aspire to compete at the international level, this is an excellent way to practice your volo and pointing skills.

A Final Note: Not many North Americans are playing this volo game. If you set your mind to it and practiced hard, you could become skilled at this event, and compete at a high level. The numbers are in your favor. Contact the United States Bocce Federation at www. bocce.com for info on how to get started.

The combination event is played one against one, with each player having four balls. The winner of the coin toss throws out the pallino and selects whether to lag or shoot in the first frame. The player not lagging will be the shooter in the first frame. The players will alternate roles in the second, third, and fourth frames, i.e. the lagger becomes the shooter, and the shooter becomes the lagger. In the fifth frame, players do not alternate roles. The player lagging in the fourth frame will lag the balls in the fifth frame. The players then alternate roles in the sixth, seventh, and eighth frames.

The pallino will be thrown by the same player for two consecutive frames, even if the player is the shooter in a frame. The first player throwing the pallino will throw in frames 1, 2, 5, and 6. The other player will throw the pallino in frames 3, 4, 7, and 8.

Points are scored as follows:

After the pallino comes to rest within the box, a 70 cm radius circle is drawn by the opponent using the center of the pallino as the center of the circle. If the pallino comes to rest less than 70 cm from the side, the center of the circle is moved laterally toward the middle of the court so that a full circle can be drawn. In this case, the pallino remains in place where it came to rest, offset from the center of the circle. The lagger rolls a ball and must land completely within the circle. If the ball is invalid, the player lags again. All invalid balls are removed from play. The lagger receives one point for each ball completely within the circle, and two points for a ball landing within one half of a centimeter from the pallino ("biberon"). When the first valid ball is within the circle the pallino is removed, a 50 cm arc is drawn, and the shooter attempts to knock the ball out of the circle. The shooter will continue to shoot until a valid hit is made. After a valid hit, the lagger will roll another ball. The shooter receives one point for each ball knocked completely out of the circle, and two points if the shooter's ball remains completely within the circle ("carreau"). If the lagger failed on all four attempts to make a point, one of the lagger's balls is placed in the center of the circle to provide a target for the shooter. Also, if the lagger is out of balls, the shooter may attempt a maximum of two shots on the pallino. If the pallino is knocked out of the circle, the shooter receives two points for each hit.

{This unofficial summary of the F.I.B. regulations was prepared by the United States Bocce Federation. It is intended only to be an abbreviated guide to the combination event. The complete text of the official F.I.B. ITR must be used for additional information or resolution of questions.}

Chapter 13
Bocce & The Special Olympics ████████████

Bocce is the fastest growing sport in Special Olympics. First off, anyone who can roll a ball can play. Secondly, as athletes age, becoming less able to participate in more rigorous sports like track and field and soccer, they often opt for a smooth transition to bocce. I volunteered as a boccc referee for two Special Olympics World Games, and it was a hectic job. Not only did we have spirited competition among athletes from all over the world, but we were bombarded with questions from coaches of other sports asking how to get their athletes started with bocce.

In 1995, New Haven, Connecticut played host to 500,000 people for the Special Olympics World Summer Games. More than 7000 athletes, and teams from 140 countries gathered there with 30 countries competing in bocce. Bocce Commissioner Marie Bedard, along with tireless assistants Jack Hogan and Roger Lord, did yeoman work assembling a bocce committee and putting together a first-class competition.

A few friends of mine and I jumped at the opportunity to become part of these World Games. We made regular trips to Waterbury, Connecticut where we learned the rules and officiating mechanics, and worked with Special Olympians. We not only became bocce officials in good standing, but we shared a very special experience with truly special athletes.

There were gala opening and closing ceremonies at the Yale Bowl, a parade of tall ships, and numerous festivals and cultural activities. President and Mrs. Clinton opened the games, and celebrities from Arnold Schwarzenegger to supermodel Kathy Ireland made appearances.

The Special Olympics movement continues to change the way society views people with mental and physical disabilities. There are no head starts, no "do-overs," no special time-outs. These athletes have the same opportunities and hardships as any other people participating in high-level competitions.

The Special Olympics Summer Games represented the largest sporting event on the planet in 1995. This is particularly impressive when you ponder the program's modest beginnings. Started in 1963 by Eunice Kennedy Shriver, it was a summer day camp for people with mental retardation. She hosted the first event in her backyard in Rockville, Maryland, and the competitors ranged from age 8 to 80. Just five years later, the first World Games were held at Soldier Field in Chicago with 1000 athletes from 26 states and Canada competing. Today, Special Olympics chapters are operating in all 50 states and more than 145 countries.

Besides bocce, World Games competition include a wide range of sports including aquatics, badminton, basketball, bowling, cycling, equestrian events, football (soccer), golf, gymnastics, power weightlifting, rollerskating, sailing, softball, table tennis, tennis, track & field, and volleyball. Many of the events include *unified teams* -- events that pair Special Olympians with athletes without mental retardation.

Bocce first became a World Games event in 1991 with 41 athletes competing. The summer of 1995 saw 151 athletes take part in singles, doubles, unified, and other bocce events. There were teams from all over the world including South Africa, New Zealand, Bahamas, Bermuda, Jamaica, France, Iceland, Spain, Switzerland, Lebanon, and the United States. It is obvious that the number of bocce participants will continue to mushroom in the future. The sport is as well suited for the Special Olympics as it is for backyard lawn games and advanced tournament play. If you can roll a ball, you can play.

Athletes with various degrees of physical and mental challenges compete extremely well. One legally blind bocce player sported binoculars strapped around his neck. He first lined up the shot, peering through the binoculars, then let them hang from his neck as he rolled each shot. After the release, he again reached for the optical aids to track the ball to its target.

For the first time, people with mental retardation served among the more than 50 officials for the bocce competition. More than 600 dedicated volunteers ran the event, coordinating game times, officials, bus schedules, meals, and everything else involved in an event of such magnitude. It was an uplifting experience seeing so many selfless people in one place, generously giving of themselves. According to other officials and spectators, the same was true at the other sports venues (approximately 45,000 volunteers in all). The positive atmosphere and harmony that pervaded the events proved that these special athletes not only bring out their best talent for world class competition...they bring out the best in all those around them.

In 1999 I again volunteered as a bocce official as the games moved to Raleigh-Durham, North Carolina. After another wonderful experience at these games, I wrote the following article, and reprint it here with permission.

****

Everybody loves the Special Olympics World Games...I mean, what's not to love? Aren't the games a positive experience for all

*1999 SO World Games opening
ceremonies - NC State University*

those athletes with mental and physical disabilities? Don't the events showcase the successes of participants with mental retardation - a condition that, years ago, relegated them to desolate lives in dehumanizing institutions?

Eunice Shriver Kennedy started the Special Olympics movement, and these World Games have blossomed into one of the largest sporting events on the planet. The 1999 World Games in North Carolina featured appearances by Arnold Schwarzenegger and Maria Shriver. Billy Crystal served as M.C. for the gala opening ceremonies. Maya Angelou inspired with a reading, NBA star Grant Hill addressed the athletes, Stevie Wonder entertained and Kathy Ireland, well, she was just Kathy Ireland, and that was enough.

Host cities love the competition because it can pump $50 million into the local economy. Big name sponsors see Special Olympics as worthwhile too - the North Carolina landscape was dotted with golden arches, Coke bottles, and M&M's. These and other corporate sponsors like Bank America and General Motors helped foot the estimated $35 million bill for the event. Everybody knows that these companies are trying to better position themselves in the World Market, but the general sentiment is "bless them, anyway" (besides, all that money is "chump change" compared to the Superbowl and the Olympics.

All those volunteers believe in the Games, too. Thirty-five thousand of them converged on the Raleigh Durham area and parked cars, controlled crowds, housed athletes, fed everyone, and worked tirelessly to make the event a success. It made me snicker at the thought of our Massachusetts high school programs that make community service a graduation requirement - as if you could mandate caring.

And for many athletes from developing countries, the World Games represent the experience of a lifetime. In some third world countries retardation is believed to be a curse, and children so inflicted might be abandoned or even poisoned by their parents. At the World Games many get a chance to see how the "other half" lives, experiencing for the first time living conditions of the high-tech world. For some, their first encounter with an escalator was at the Raleigh Durham Airport, and they boarded with much trepidation. We heard of athletes who washed their hands and face and then drank the water, and others who consumed the unfinished juice in glasses left on the breakfast table. Athletes from tropical zones asked that the air conditioning be turned off. And others even thought they were to draw their water from the pond behind their host family's home.

Despite all the obvious benefits I was surprised to find another side to the Special Olympics story. I was in North Carolina's Triangle area to officiate the bocce competition. Long a passion of mine, bocce is one of the fastest growing sports in Special Olympics, since anyone who can roll a ball can play. As many athletes from track and field and other more physically demanding sports age, they make the transition to bocce.

It was at the bocce venue on the grounds of the picturesque Fearrington Village that we first heard the controversy. A newspaper headline read "Some advocates for mainstreaming assail the games." Some think the Special Olympics movement is counter-productive to the efforts for mainstreaming, instead perpetuating the stereotype of the mentally retarded as poor unfortunates deserving of pity.

And since the event is almost exclusively for the retarded, it only undermines the work being done toward inclusion. These critics maintain that even the adjective "special" is condescending. I read the article with great interest...it hadn't occurred to me that there might even be debate about the benefits of The Games.

Bocce venue - Fearrington
Village, NC - World Games 1999

Nancy Weiss is executive director of the Baltimore based TASH, "an international association of people with disabilities...fighting for a society in which inclusion for all people in all aspects of society is the norm." Weiss maintains that "all that (Special Olympics) time and energy and fundraising would do more good if put into integrated activities." Labeling Special Olympics a segregated event, Weiss and TASH continue to hammer home the same, consistent message, promoting inclusive recreational activities.

Other critics point out that we should be rewarding academic achievements as well as the athletic. We ought to recognize the efforts made at surmounting what are, for many, the daunting tasks of developing independence, learning to cook, keep house, and manage money. And many parents reject the term special - what future opportunities might be lost once their child is labeled as special needs? The more you segregate, the more you foster separate and unequal. There are Special Boys Scout troops in some areas. Why wouldn't these boys just be part of the existing scout troops? "That way," maintains Weiss, "they'd have friends and role models with and without disabilities."

There is a whole lot of hugging going on at Special Olympics, and some see this as demeaning to the athletes. College students and other volunteers, they allege, are recruited as "professional huggers." It's pretty obvious that no one should get in the habit of hugging strangers, but that is exactly what often takes place as volunteers and athletes embrace at the conclusion of each competition.

Special Olympics creates many divisions so that athletes are competing against others of nearly the same skill level. This makes for many gold, silver, and bronze medal winners. One newspaper headline read "These athletes are so good, they all walk away with medals." The true nature of competition is that it creates more losers than winners.

All those Division I college basketball teams want to be NCAA champs, but only 64 make the tournament, and only one survives March Madness to earn the bragging rights. Isn't the Special Olympics medal situation a kind of inflation? If so many are awarded, what is the value of a medal? Isn't this demeaning to the athletes? Shouldn't they be able to compete and be afforded the dignity of taking the risk of coming up empty?

All of these criticisms made sense to me - but, in North Carolina I felt that I was part of something positive. At the 1995 World Summer Games, in Connecticut, my first, I was struck by the fact that those with mental retardation were the "whole show." They were the athletes, the coaches, officials, volunteers, and the entertainment. What's more inclusive than that? And the Special Olympics competition is moving toward "unified" events, which pair athletes who have retardation with those who do not, but who have similar skill levels.

Don't these events help raise consciousness, change people's attitudes about mental retardation? The athletes love to compete and to meet people from different countries and to try to be the best that they can be. Don't all of us who enjoy competition do just that

271

- try to find a level at which we can compete and have fun? The reason I play hoop Thursday nights with the "old bucks" is because I can't compete with the young kids anymore. And wasn't one of the reasons I attended a small New England college so that I could play Division II baseball rather than take the chance of getting lost in the shuffle at a major university? Special Olympics represents a level at which athletes with disabilities can compete, have fun, and experience the positives and negatives of that competition. Placed alongside inclusive recreational activities, Special Olympics is a plus. Miami YMCA Executive Director Anna Necheles claims that "Special Olympics really makes a huge difference in people's lives, and it shows the world what these athletes can do." The games give athletes a start, and they can go on to parks and recreation leagues as the next step. Parents of an athlete from Ireland talked about how their daughter played in the town basketball league, but was a "bench warmer." But in the World Summer Games she was a full-time player and her team won the gold. "She found an arena where she could excel," says Necheles "and this can only have positive carry-over effects."

Trying to clarify my thoughts on the Special Olympics experience, I reflected on my experience in North Carolina. I saw athletes treated as adults and always afforded basic human dignity. I didn't see the so-called infantilization of adults with disabilities. I saw volunteerism in its purest form. People from all over the globe converged on the Triangle area and gave of themselves. Rico Daniele, owner of an Italian deli and Richard Calvanese, a self-employed CPA closed down their Massachusetts businesses to serve as volunteer officials. Kim Davis, a teacher from Boone, North Carolina, revamped her vacation schedule to be there.

I saw humor. When Wayne Boggs of Nebraska won the coin toss and I gave him his choice of red or green bocce balls, there was a short pause as he considered his options. Then with a big grin he decided "I'll take red...same color as my pick-up." And I saw tears. When Wayne needed one more point to win the gold medal, he looked toward the heavens, and in a poignant moment, called out "Mama, it's up to you now." The tears belonged to Kim Davis.

I witnessed intense athletic endeavor and tension. At the softball venue in a game between Iowa and Venezuela, both benches emptied after a collision between a base runner and fielder. It appeared to observers that an ugly international incident might be at hand - but both teams merely wanted to congratulate hard play and to make certain that everyone was unhurt.

I saw determination. Athletes are charged with signing the scorecard after each bocce contest. I watched the Jamaican, Coy Barker, take the pen in his hand made inflexible by cerebral palsy and begin what became the arduous task of writing his name. It seemed to take him longer to autograph the scorecard than it did to play the game, but he persisted. Coy re-adjusted the pen in his hand several times, doodled to get the ink flowing, made several false starts, and labored over each cursive letter - but finally, satisfied with the result, proudly handed me the signed card.

And I encountered some poor sportsmanship on the part of athletes and coaches. Why shouldn't the negative aspects of sports be here as well as the positive?

The next World Summer Games are slated for Ireland in 2003. It will be the first time the games will be hosted outside the USA. They'll use Dublin University and Point Theatre and other venues. Will I be there? I'm not sure what to make of all these criticisms of Special Olympics. Most make good sense to me. They come from bright and experienced people - those in the trenches, so to speak. Special Olympics organizers need to listen and to work more closely with these well-meaning critics. But, my instincts tell me that I was part of something very special in North Carolina. It is something I definitely want more of, and, like Arnold Schwarzenegger, "I'll be back!" if they'll have me.

****

Epilogue: The 2003 Games were a big success (organizers used mostly European referees, so I did not attend). Marie Bedard, the tireless worker for Special Olympics bocce sent this report to *The Joy of Bocce Weekly*...

"Well the Special Olympics World Games are over and with the greatest success. We had 204 athletes from 40 countries. We offered 5 events and 66 divisions and played 464 games. Organizers and participants were very happy, since we did not have to worry about weather. Our indoor courts were 'tops'. The scoreboards were in the colors of the balls, red and green, and included the names of the countries that were playing at the time."

Ed Crozier (Texas) updated us too...

"My daughter and I got to go to the Special Olympics World Games in Ireland. She was an athlete/official (in Bocce) and I was her mentor.

The courts were inside the RDS (Royal Dublin Society) in south Dublin. They were elevated slightly to allow the courts to be made flat. The court size was 12' x 60' which is the standard size for Special Olympics. The surface was an Astroturf type of grass with sand. It ran quite well. I thought the balls would roll like on a Putt Putt golf course, but the carpet and sand slowed them down to be comparable to a well manicured golf green.

World Games 2003 - Royal Dublin Society - Ed Crozier photo

We had approximately 200 athletes - two days of classifications followed by a full week of competition. The last afternoon the officials were teamed up with the athletes and the coaches were the officials. What fun."

Note: Visit http://www.specialolympics.org. The comprehensive web site includes everything from background information to finding a program near you, to signing on as a volunteer or coach.

Special Olympics Oath
Let me win.
But if I cannot win
Let me be brave in the
attempt.

Regional games played in an open field with Backyard Bocce courts

Chapter 14
The Best Of The Joy of Bocce Weekly ▬▬

Background

In 2002, I began launching a weekly electronic newsletter. Initially emailed to about 1000 bocce aficionados, circulation quickly increased by nearly ten-fold. Connecting bocce players from around North America (with a smattering of international subscribers as well) the publication continues to flourish.

Early on, we got noticed by email publishing industry professionals. Janet Roberts, who writes a popular column for electronic newsletter publishers (Ezine-Tips.com), made reference to "Mario Pagnoni, who publishes an infectiously enthusiastic email newsletter called the Joy of Bocce Weekly..."

Writing in Best Ezines Issue #115 - June 5, 2002, Ms. Roberts said...

"If you don't play bocce (an Italian bowling game), you'll want to run out and find the nearest court after reading this enthusiastic ezine. Mario Pagnoni claims not to be a bocce pro, but you wouldn't know it from his devotion to the sport. Each issue of the HTML ezine (with graphics and colors) features his personal comment on some aspect of the game and its players, highlights of coming tournaments and detailed evaluations of new bocce products. The ezine also fosters a feeling of community in the bocce world by including reader comments and a photo section each week. Whether you learned to play in your Uncle Joe's backyard court or you're looking for a new sport to master, Joy of Bocce will point you in the right direction."

Initially, I was unsure about maintaining a weekly deadline. One reader, an ezine publisher himself, cautioned me about how ambitious an undertaking a weekly would become. He was right of course. But it has been a labor of love.

My primary goal was, and still is, to promote the game we love, and to be a voice for unifying the sport. It irritates me that horseshoes (a good game, but one that can't hold a candle to ours) is so well standardized while North American bocce still struggles to get to that next level.

Joy of Bocce Weekly subscribers took to the ezine right away...

"I think your weekly e-mag is a wonderful idea and will go a long way to further popularize this excellent sport that combines social as well as athletic skills. I look forward to the next edition." Sal Fauci - Endicott, NY

"I wish you well on this new endeavor. Anything anyone can do to help promote the sport helps fulfill the goals of the United States Bocce Federation."
Donna Allen - USBF

"Thanks for keeping the game alive. You will always have support from here."
Rich Mazzulla - Elmwood Park, IL

"I welcome your *Joy of Bocce Weekly*. I'm the Texas Special Olympics Director of Bocce Competition." Ed Crozier

"Hey Mario--- Great newsletter! Keep 'em coming." Jeff Jernstedt - Portland, Oregon

"Your Ezine was a welcome surprise for the New Year, and I think a good idea." Stan Stanton - Las Vegas, NV

Referring to the standard "opt out" language for ezines, Peter Ferris of Coweta, Oklahoma wrote...

"I thought 'bocce' and 'unsubscribe' were mutually exclusive! You shouldn't use them in the same sentence!"

Ray DiCecca of Wilmington, MA offered...

"I very much enjoy your weekly newsletter, and look forward to reading my e-mail every Monday morning, knowing that the latest "Joy Of Bocce" will be waiting for me. It's great to have one location collecting as much information as you do on such an enjoyable subject."

DiCecca inquired about back issues which prompted me to implement an archive system at www.joyofbocce.com (Back Issues).

You can "opt in" to receive *The Joy of Bocce Weekly* by visiting www.joyofbocce.com and adding your email address to any of a number of subscription links sprinkled throughout the web site. You will then receive an email that says, in effect, "So you want to start receiving the weekly ezine on bocce. Is that right?" Only after you respond to this email in the affirmative will your email address be added to our "house list".

YES you can "opt out" at any time, and NO we won't give away or sell your personal info (you can opt in just by giving your email address, no other info required). Your subscription will bring you bocce stories, comments and suggestions on bocce play from readers around the globe, tournament listings, and easy access to our most popular "Photos of the Week" feature.

Bocce Quotes Of The Week

A regular column called Bocce Quote of the Week became an instant hit with readers. Following are a couple favorites...

It's Easy!

Our Monday morning outdoor bocce season is often hosted by yours truly. My wife, pictured on the home page of www.joyofbocce. com (displaying outstanding bocce form, I might add), runs a family daycare home. The kids always know when it's bocce day. They come outside for recess and chant "Bocce! Bocce! Bocce!" lead by four-year-old Ryan Hamilton. As a matter of fact, if you ask two-year-old Jacob "What day is today?" on any given morning he'll shout "Bocce Day!" without hesitation.

The adult players arrive at 9:00 am. We have coffee and pastry, then play games separated by short breaks for more libations, "trash talking" (we believe we've taken trash talking to a new level), and more food. Ryan, already an avid sports fan (NE Patriots, Boston Red Sox), became so enamored of the game that he asked for a bocce set for Christmas. Santa delivered. Recently he taught his parents and sister how to play. "It's easy," he said. "First you eat. Then you roll some balls. Then you eat again!"

✱✱

Intermission

We are constantly looking for "new blood" for our Monday morning bocce sessions here in Massachusetts. Most of us are retirees, and we try to recruit younger players. Recently, we've added some twenty- and thirty-year-olds to the fold. We play several games, enjoying coffee and pastry between matches. After a recent match, 86 year-old Del Bracci, a former National Super Senior Downhill Ski champ said "Nice game... time for an intermission."

One of the "young pups", an athletic, energetic type and first-time bocce player, chimed in with, "Intermission? For crying out loud - the entire game's an intermission!"

Okay, bocce might not be a cardiovascular workout. But the pastime's gentle exercise, friendly competition, and camaraderie is among the finest mental health programs. And never underestimate its value as a lifetime sport - one you'll not have to abandon as you age.

Del the ski champ - when he got to the final heat for the gold medal,the other two competitors in the running had been members of the Romanian Olympic team - they had to settle for silver and bronze

****

Close, But No Cigar!

During one hotly contested match, one team made a great roll, the ball coming to rest touching the pallino. It was Tom's turn next, and he never hits, preferring to lag no matter how close the other guy's point. He rolled deftly, making a terrific shot – his ball also "kissing" the pallino.

We examined the situation, trying to wedge a credit card or dollar bill between the balls. No doubt about it. It was a "dead heat."

We told Tom to roll again, because, although he had tied the other team's point, he hadn't beaten it. Confused, Tom ambled down the court to take a look for himself. He peered from one angle, then took another vantage point. He squinted, scratched his head, and finally spoke. "Sure, they're both touching" he announced..."but mine is definitely closer!"

****

Chess/Bocce

When I introduced bocce to my friend Walter, he took to it right away. A competitive, athletic type, Walt likes softball, racquetball, and karate. He particularly enjoys the strategic aspects of bocce, like leaving a ball in front to block, tapping the pallino to another, more advantageous position, and thinking ahead a move or two. This cerebral aspect of our sport is missed by most beginners. They enjoy playing. They begin to get better at the sport. But, once they see the broader picture - that the game involves tactics and maneuvers that require advance planning, they are hooked.

Sure, you still need good touch and finesse, some occasional brute force, and even a little luck, but this is a pensive person's pastime. "This game is a lot like chess" says Walter. "The problem is, I know where I want to put the pieces, but I can't always get them there."

****

The Joy of Bocce and the Arts

Long-time promoters of bocce, Rico Daniele and I had similar questions when asked to run a bocce event in the Arts District of Chattanooga, Tennessee. "They play bocce in Tennessee?" asked Rico, while I countered with "You mean to tell me they have an Arts District in Chattanooga?" Surprisingly (and fortunately), the answer to both questions is Yes! And Dr. Charles (Tony) Portera is the man largely responsible. A transplanted Mississippian, Portera is one of the South's leading cancer surgeons. The tall, handsome 63 year-old has a staunch passion for medicine and the arts, an unwavering vision about what he wants for his city, and a firm grasp on his roots. Together with his wife Mary and their family, he has conceived and developed the Bluff View Arts District, a classic conclave of cafes, gardens, museums and galleries.

Nestled in one of the city's finest historic areas, Bluff View features bed and breakfast in elegantly restored homes (circa 1900), gourmet dining in any of several restaurants (fresh made pastas, pastries, and chocolates), and culture in the River Gallery and the outdoor Sculpture Garden featuring local as well as nationally known artists' work.

Gazing over all that comprises the Arts District, including the gorgeous, well-manicured bocce court overlooking the Tennessee River, renowned oncologist Portera declared "I deal with death every day - I did this for joy."

*Bronze of Dr. Portera and
grandchild - Bluff View Arts District*

Readers' Feedback

The ezine serves as a sounding board for players who make comments, ask questions, and offer suggestions.

Journeyman player Dr. Angel Cordano's vote of confidence read… "Congratulations for the enjoyable *Joy of Bocce* that I eagerly read every week. You are doing a great service to our sport by exposing what's going on all over the US."

Sometimes there are questions I can answer myself…

Steve Kahn from Banning, CA …

"Us old codgers are having a mild argument. One side says that all team members shoot from one end of the court, then all walk to the other end and shoot again. This is obviously a must for singles.

The other side says that for two-person teams one member of each team is at each end. For four-person teams two members of each team are at each end. In either case, nobody walks. Which is right?"

My answer…

Whichever way you decide to play is right. There is no hard and fast rule for this. I prefer a little walking to get some exercise. Also, there is more camaraderie when all of the players are at one end…and, when walking end to end, you play every frame instead of every other one.

The only time we stay at one end is when we play 4 vs. 4. Two teammates are stationed at each end, rolling two balls each. An alternative would be to keep all 8 players at one end, roll one ball each, and walk end to end.

This weekend I visited Baltimore, Maryland's Little Italy - see This Week's Photos. They were playing 6 vs. 6 and using 12 bocce balls. Three teammates were stationed at each end – no walking – and each player rolled 2 balls, making it possible to score 6 points in a single frame. Games were played to a score of 12.

Sometimes there are questions a reader can answer...

Someone asked about a game with 3 players in an "every man for himself" or "cut-throat" mode. What would determine the order of play in such a match?

Self proclaimed "Bocce Bum" Ben Musolf of California shed a little light on the question...

"We play cut-throat all the time. The rotation of play is as follows. First you determine who goes 1st, 2nd, and 3rd. Then it is the same as regular bocce. Whoever is farthest away from the pallino goes. We play up to 30 points where the closest ball gets 3 pts, second gets 2 pts and the third gets 1 point. Therefore, you can score up to 6 points in the round if you have the three closest. We only use three balls each though."

I usually add my two cents worth...{my comments in brackets}

{Thanks Ben. This clears up the rotation of play with three players. Whichever of the three is farthest away must roll the next ball. The scoring is unorthodox in several ways. Score three, two, and one points for the three closest balls instead of just one point each...and more than one player can score in a round – in fact all three could score...interesting. Now we'll need a scoreboard to track three players' totals. A final thought...we need a better term than "cut-throat" for this style of play.}

Another question answered by a reader...

"Do you have to roll your last balls when you have the game winning point and the other team is out of balls? Can you drop them at your feet?"

I've seen players toss their remaining balls a couple feet in front of the foul line to signify that they are done playing and the match is won. If they were to play a ball they might "sell the point" as they say. That is, they might knock an opponent's ball closer or hit the pallino and give away the point (I don't know where the selling part comes in).

Mike Conti of the United States Bocce Federation supplied the answer...

"When Yogi Berra made the comment 'It's not over until it's over' he also meant when it's over it is over. When you win you want to celebrate and thank your opponents for a good game, not drop balls in front of their face - that's like rubbing it in."

Sometimes we get questions that evoke multiple answers from subscribers...

"How do you handle league play when one team is short-handed (e.g. when only three of your four team players show up for the match)?"

The background...

Many leagues station four players (two teammates for each team) at each end of the court, each player rolling two balls. They prefer this to all eight players (both teams) crowding one end, and rolling just one ball each.

Now, the short-handed team will have two players at one end, but only one at the other end. If this player rolls four balls, he gains an advantage over his two opponents who roll just two balls each.

Lots of readers weighed in on this, allowing the rest of us to consider the options and choose what's best for us.

Several suggested using a "walker." This is when one of the three players rolls two balls with a partner on one end, then walks to the other end to roll two balls with his other teammate. The walker plays both ends of the court, but only plays two balls at each end like everybody else.

Other readers preferred to "burn" a ball or two for the person who plays singles. The solo guy can't play four balls, only two or three. That's the penalty for being short-handed.

Still another offered…

"At our club when a team is short-handed, the walker is picked by the captain of the other team. It works quite well and is a just penalty for the team that is missing a player, since it is logical that the 'worst' player of the team will be designated to walk.

This may avoid any possible intentional arrangement by a team to come with only 3 players."

{In softball we use a "courtesy runner" when a player reaches base safely, but is injured or can't continue to run the bases. In the leagues that let the other team pick the courtesy runner, there may be hard feelings. Some tactless coach always seems to yell out something like "Let that fat guy run!"}

Tom McNutt of Boccemon.com chipped in with another creative solution…

"We play that the whole team has to be walkers. Person #1 and #2 start at end A. After the first frame, Person #1 goes down to end B to join #3. After the second frame #3 goes to end A to play with teammate #1. For the fourth frame #1 and #2 are down at end B. The team of four plays as normal with no walkers. This type of rotation slightly punishes the threesome, as they never quite get used to either end, and yet gives both teams the same number of balls. Playing an entire match one ball short isn't a handicap... it is crippling!"

{In our Ken Waldie Senior Sports Circuit here in Massachusetts we experimented with the various methods, finally settling on using a walker. Since we have three games in our league matches, we rotate the walker (each of the three players gets to be the walker in one game).

McNutt's rotating walker system is a good one. But our players (ages 50 and over) kept getting mixed up (frequent "senior moments"), forgetting who just walked down one end, and whose turn it was to travel to the other.}

We get comments that inform...

I found that many of our readers dabble in other outdoor games as well as bocce. Quite a few subscribers are avid pétanque players.

Jan and Louis Toulon of Toulon Imports and the Pétanque Mariniere Club of San Rafael, California enjoy pétanque or boules, as it is sometimes called. Similar to bocce played with small metal balls, I learned the game while in Holland and found it quite enjoyable. The only complaint I had was that it was often difficult to tell which ball belonged to which team because the variation in color is not striking. You really had to pay attention to which ball was tossed by which player.

Tom Grow from The TX Hill Country says "We rotate Croquet, Horseshoes, Bocce & Badminton - Bocce always dominates (goes better with wine)."

We learned about people in carpeted office buildings playing bocce on their breaks and lunch hours. The down time is too short for them to get to the gym and back, and the brief diversion (mental and even a tad physical) is just what the doctor ordered. One advocate of the practice declared it perfect for "high powered business types who want to compete, but don't want to work up a sweat."

We get compliments...

Jim Mancini of Visalia, CA writes...

"I'm about halfway through your book – I skip around – and it is terrific. Everything I wanted to know and then some. And you write clearly and concisely."

Sometimes we get compliments and a feeling that we made a difference...

Dick Gomez from Northern California...

"Thanks for the great newsletter and web site. I also have to thank you for your book, *The Joy of Bocce*. My wife read it at least six years ago, and it changed her game completely. She was a one night a week, play for fun, wine, and food type player, but after she read your book, she became more interested in the game, and has become a most excellent lagger. She's a tournament champion, and still retains her passion for the game (as do I)."

There are always questions about court construction.

The award for Best Advice to a Prospective Court Builder goes to Mike Hoban of Raleigh, NC. Says Hoban, "Build it and they will come...with beverages."

We get opinions...

"The US has innumerable players scattered all over, playing almost independently on their local turf and it is time to get together in order to become a world power. I would like to see that we play with similar size and weight bocce balls of 107 mm and 920 grams, since those are the official measurements at world level competition."

We get complaints...

"Why can't we get TV exposure for our game so that we can reach a wider audience?"

{Television exposure is just what this game needs. There is a groundswell of activity with this wonderful sport that needs to be harnessed and pointed in the right direction. A couple years back I officiated a big money tournament hosted by Las Vegas' Golden Nugget Casino. Organizer Phil Ferrari came up short in his bid for TV coverage after negotiating with ESPN and Fox. The championship game between a veteran club from Toronto and a team that featured Dr. Angel Cordano and three fine young players from the San Francisco area was a thing of beauty. Every player made the shot that he needed to make in virtually every situation. If televised nationally, this match would have done more to promote the game's popularity than any single event I can imagine.}

Sometimes we get the word out on bocce happenings...

The Dating Story (which airs on The Learning Channel) filmed a "bocce date" in New York City. We alerted readers to the episode's airing date and time, and later offered this recap.

The episode was filmed at Washington Square Park and several boules and bocce players who are "regulars" at the park were happy to coach the couple (and get in front of the camera).

Caroline, from Hoboken, New Jersey, and Carmine, of Staten Island, had a passing familiarity with bocce.

Carmine, a 28 year-old letter carrier and Caroline, a 31 year-old real estate agent studying nursing in the evenings, seemed to hit it off pretty well on this, their first date.

Before the date, Carmine's friends teased him with the following banter...

"She's gonna whip your butt in bocce."
"Maybe her school's got a bocce team."
"Yea, maybe she's a pro."
"Maybe she's putting herself through school with bocce."
"I think I read about her in Sports Illustrated."

Caroline just ended a relationship and is "holding out for the right person." She aptly described their dating scenario as "an interactive game of bocce."

One of Caroline's friends wisely counseled her that "Bocce will show if you are compatible or not."

Although they seemed a little confused about how to play and how to keep score, it was obvious that Caroline and Carmine enjoyed the game and each other's company.

When they parted company, Caroline wrote her phone number on a Post-it note and handed it to her date. True to his word, Carmine called her. The TV episode closed with Caroline's statement that "I can't wait for our second date."

We sometimes review other interesting bocce web sites...

While cruising around the Internet recently I came across (http://bocce.baltimore.md.us).

The webmaster (Thom LaCosta) has created an entertaining and well organized bocce site containing details on Baltimore's bocce action as well as general information on the sport.

I particularly like the web site's section on the History of Bocce. Like other historical accounts (and lore) it quotes Sir Francis Drake who is purported to have said of the rapidly advancing Spanish Armada…"First we finish the game, then we deal with the Armada." But this is the first time I have come across the following light-hearted and very amusing account credited to Michael Kilian of the Chicago Tribune…

"Some historians claim bocce dates back 7,000 years. The Egyptians played it when they weren't struggling with pyramid stones, and the Romans picked it up from them (I don't think Cleopatra did, however, as it's not a game you can play in bed).

The barbarians within the Roman Empire took a liking to it – the Gauls producing a French version called "boule." The English, who never quite got the hang of things, turned it into the tacky pastime you see on television's Championship Bowling.

Unlike Championship Bowling, bocce is not a game of roll, slam, crash, rack and have another brewski. It's a true sport involving skill, finesse, strategy and cunning."

Best of all – we reprint photos…

Subscribers from all over the continent (and sometimes Europe) send photos of their bocce venues, court construction or tournament action. We change the photos on the web site each week and feature a regular ezine column titled "Photos of the Week." By far the most popular part of the publications, these pictures provide insight into the world of bocce – different types of courts, kinds of constructions, and styles of play. We love viewing other people's bocce courts, and we enjoy seeing others reveling in the joy of bocce.

And finally,

Sometimes we even reprint great works of literature...

Bocce lover and poet William "Pete" Gallagher sent this literary treat in honor of his friend Sal Fauci's bocce league in Endicott, NY.

The friends get together weekly to play at Sal's backyard court and to enjoy each other's company. In Gallagher's nicely crafted piece, the sheer joy of bocce shines through. {That's Sal with the scissors in photo of the ribbon cutting ceremony.}

Sal Fauci's bocce ribbon cutting ceremony

Ode to the Bocce Boys of the Summer of 2001

By William "Pete" Gallagher

On July twenty-fifth of two thousand and one,
A coin was flipped and the games were begun.
Bocce was started by our friend, Sal,
Except when he's playing, he's also our pal.

293

The court was a gift from his beautiful wife,
"Mary A" as she's known, the joy of his life.
Sal labored and toiled to make the court right,
With much soil and sand, it made quite a sight.

"Now all we need is some players," said Sal,
So he called on his friends who weren't in jail.
There was Lou and Bob, and Pete and Joe,
Bob and John and Mike Battaglino.

And so the P.M. league was formed,
Of all the rules all were informed.
On all the calls no one could fudge,
'Cause Sal let us know he was the judge.

At first sight it appeared a motley crew,
Most of us had no clue.
But since we were athletes all,
Each strove to make his opponents fall.

There was Mike who comes from expert lineage,
Which seemed to some to give him a mini-edge.
His skillful spin was no surprise,
One day he played with drops in his eyes.

Lou can best be described as cool,
Perhaps this comes from playing pool.
Though mostly considered a competitive sort,
In defeat, he was a very good sport.

Bob Christie is a neighbor dear,
Built a screen the court to clear.
But instead of Crowley's products fine,
Sal chose to serve Italian wine.

Joe is truly the quiet type,
With his ever present distinctive pipe.
When calls were close, Joe had no fear,
He could tell which ball was near.

Big John Simek is usually kind,
A gentler person is hard to find.
Except when he's rooting against you,
Or displacing your ball right on cue.

Bob Strollo rolls the ball low,
Gives to your ball quite a blow.
Always called upon to measure,
To the league he's surely a treasure.

Pete leaned on Mike quite a bit,
To some teasing, had to submit.
Enjoyed the wine and stogies – true,
But showed that the Irish can play bocce, too.

Now I've come to the end of my story,
It's true we all strove for glory.
But in this game on the court of clay,
Only one team could win the day.

But all in all we must admit,
We thank good Sal, he started it.
And as we look forward to the fall,
We will remember Bocce, we had a ball.

About the Author

Mario Pagnoni is the author of several computer, education, and sports books. His *The Complete Home Educator* (Larson, 1984) was a McGraw-Hill Book Club selection. In the foreword to that book, noted author/educator John Holt said of the computer information… "It is by far the clearest explanation of this difficult and rather forbidding subject that I have seen. Indeed, it is one of the clearest explanations I have ever seen of any scientific subject. Mario is a superb explainer…"

Pagnoni has written for *The Boston Globe, Referee,* and numerous magazines. He also publishes the highly successful *Joy of Bocce Weekly,* an ezine connecting bocce aficionados everywhere. Find out more at www.joyofbocce.com.

A retired high school teacher and coach, he resides with his family in Methuen, Massachusetts.

Printed in the United States
95708LV00003B/208/A

9 781418 407162